insight text guide

Mark Eckersley

Away

Michael Gow

First published in 2015, reprinted in 2019, 2021, 2023, 2024.

Insight Publications Pty Ltd
3/350 Charman Road
Cheltenham VIC 3192
Australia
Tel: +61 3 8571 4950
Email: books@insightpublications.com.au

www.insightpublications.com.au

National Library of Australia Cataloguing-in-Publication entry:
Eckersley, Mark, author.
Michael Gow's Away / Mark Eckersley.
9781925134087 (paperback)
Insight text guide.
Includes bibliographical references.
For secondary school age.
Gow, Michael. Away.
Gow, Michael—Criticism and interpretation.
A822.3

Other ISBNs:
9781925175028 (digital)

Cover design: The Modern Art Production Group

Printed by Markono Print Media Pte Ltd

contents

CHARACTER MAP

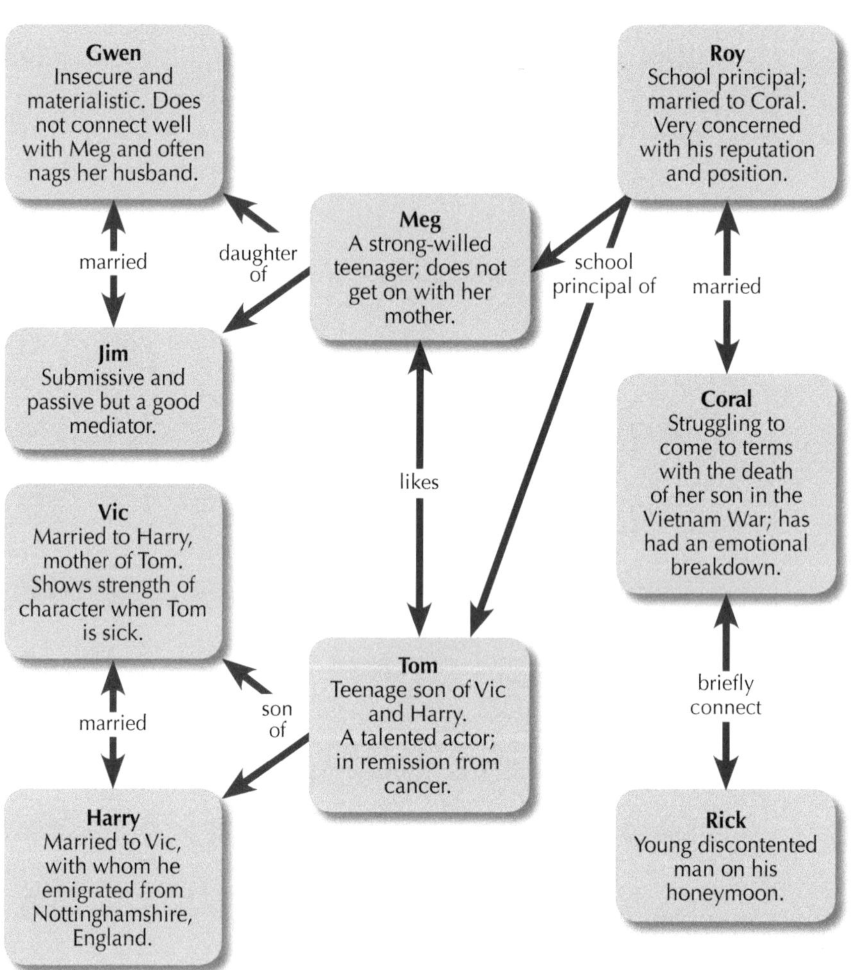

OVERVIEW

About the playwright

Michael Gow is an Australian playwright and director who was born in 1955 in Sydney. He grew up in Como in Southern Sydney and graduated from Jannali High School in 1972. He started his work in theatre at the Australian Theatre for Young People and went on to act and direct with the Sydney University Dramatic Society (SUDS) from 1973 until 1976. After graduating from Sydney University, Gow worked as an actor from 1977 to 1983 with the Nimrod Theatre Company, Thalia Theatre Company and Sydney Theatre Company. He also acted in television miniseries, such as *The Young Doctors* and *The Last Frontier*, and films including *Stir* (1980).

In 1982, Gow wrote his first play, *The Kid*, which was given a workshop reading at the Australian National Playwright's Conference and was eventually produced in 1983. This rites-of-passage play centres around a naive young boy called Donald who is confronted by the seedy side of city life. *The Kid* was followed by a television screenplay entitled *Crime of the Decade* (1984). In 1985 he wrote the play *The Astronaut's Wife*; then in 1986 his best known play, *Away*, which was first performed by the Griffin Theatre Company at the Stables Theatre in Sydney. This heralded a golden period in Gow's playwriting in the late 1980s when he wrote *On Top of the World* (1987), *Europe* (1987), *1841* (1988) and *All Stops Out* (1989).

During the 1990s, Gow wrote *Furious* (1994), *Sweet Phoebe* (1994) and *Live Acts On Stage* (1996) and also juggled his playwriting with other aspects of the theatre such as directing. He was appointed Artistic Director of the Queensland Theatre Company in 1999 and directed many acclaimed and successful productions, such as *The Fortunes of Richard Mahony* (2004; Gow's own adaptation of Henry Handel Richardson's novel), *Private Fears in Public Places* (2007), *Who's Afraid of Virginia Woolf?* (2007), *The Importance of Being Earnest* (2008), *I Am My Own*

Wife (2009), *The School of Art* and *The Crucible* (2009) and *Richard III* (2010). Gow wrote only a few plays during this period, including *Up There* (2004) and the award-winning *Toy Symphony* (2007).

After leaving the Queensland Theatre Company, Gow went on to direct productions for theatre and opera companies, including Mozart's *Don Giovanni* for Oz Opera. More recently, Gow has returned to writing plays, and *Once in Royal David's City* – which examines the onset of middle age and how the world changes when one is not paying attention to it – opened to critical success in 2014.

Synopsis

Away is a five-act drama set in Australia in 1967 and early 1968. The action centres on three Australian families and their Christmas holiday. The play opens with a school performance of Shakespeare's *A Midsummer Night's Dream*. Tom performs Puck's final speech of the play. Roy, the school's principal, commends the performances of the students and thanks people for coming.

Backstage after the show, Tom gives Meg a brooch. Gwen and Jim, Meg's mother and father, arrive and Gwen criticises the choice of play, while Jim praises Tom's performance. Jim and Gwen then argue over who has the car keys. Roy (the principal) and Coral (his wife) arrive, followed soon after by Harry and Vic (Tom's parents). They then all talk about where they are going for Christmas. Harry mentions that his family is going camping, Gwen says her family will be caravanning and Roy says he and Coral are flying to the Gold Coast. When Roy and Coral exit, Gwen mentions subtly that something happened to Roy and Coral's son, from which the audience infers that he has died recently. Harry and Vic also prepare to leave, and Tom says that he will walk home. After they leave, Gwen makes derogatory comments about Tom's family. Tom, overhearing this, returns to wish Gwen and her family a rotten holiday. Alone outside the hall, Coral talks of how the performance moved her; she reflects on the words of the play and the god-like imagery of the young actors on stage. When Roy enters, he is embarrassed by Coral's behaviour and wants to get her home as soon as possible.

Later that night, Tom arrives home and finds his father waiting up for him. Before they go to bed, Harry reminds Tom how important their forthcoming trip is for Tom's mother.

Meanwhile, Gwen is still up, organising her family's holiday packing. Meg reluctantly helps but wants her mother to stop and go to bed. After Gwen leaves the room, Jim talks to his daughter about Tom and reveals his worries that Meg may be being pulled away from her family. He asks Meg to be patient with her mother.

The action then crosses to the end of the evening at Roy and Coral's house, where Roy criticises Coral for her antisocial behaviour and points out how it undermines his position. He reminds her that they are not the only ones who have lost a son in a war. Coral agrees to try to act normally.

Later, at a luxury hotel on the Gold Coast, Coral meets and talks to Leonie and then Rick. Rick, on his honeymoon, is waiting for his wife. Coral can't help but compare Rick to her dead son. Roy arrives and ushers Coral to dinner.

The scene switches to Gwen's family, at a caravan and camping park. Gwen is carrying a Christmas tree. Meg and Jim enter. Jim is looking for a cardboard box he left in the house beside the suitcases to be packed in the car. The box contained presents for Gwen. Meg accuses her mother of intentionally leaving the box behind. Although initially Gwen denies leaving the box, eventually she admits she did so deliberately, but attacks Meg for being rude and ungrateful before she leaves. A group of campers then arrives; they want Jim to sign a petition about improvements and rules for the campground but, when they leave, Jim tears the petition up.

It is New Year's Eve at the Gold Coast hotel. Coral and Rick (the young man she met) are up on the roof talking intimately. Rick describes how his wife Susie is jealous of him spending time with Coral. Roy arrives on the roof, looking for Coral. Rick leaves and Roy threatens to send Coral to a doctor, arrange shock treatment and lock her up in an asylum.

We switch back to the caravan park. Fairies enter and stage a storm sequence. Jim and Gwen pack up everything and the Fairies and the storm wreak havoc.

Harry, Vic and Tom gather on a beach just after the storm. They are happy with the simple Christmas presents they have given one another. They seem to cherish their time together.

The storm has forced Jim, Gwen and Meg to leave their caravan site and they have ended up at the same beach where Vic, Harry and Tom are staying. Vic and Harry tell Jim and Gwen about the beach and the surroundings. They see a woman in a kaftan and Vic comments on how mysterious the woman looks. Gwen launches into a tirade about people being mad and unmotivated. Vic takes Gwen for a walk. Harry talks to Jim, and reveals to him that Tom has terminal cancer and is in remission. Vic and Gwen return and Vic invites Gwen and Jim to the Campers' amateur night. Harry and Vic depart and Gwen and Jim are left to ponder the news of Tom's terminal illness.

Tom reveals to Meg that he knows the strange 'artistic' woman in the kaftan is in fact Coral, who has run away from her husband on New Year's Eve. Tom then makes advances towards Meg and asks her to have sex with him. Meg politely rejects these advances. Tom then tells Meg that he knows that he has a terminal illness but asks her not to tell his parents that he knows how serious his condition is.

Later that evening at the Campers' amateur night, Tom performs a playlet with Coral. It tells the story of a sailor who drowns, becomes a ghost and falls in love with a woman. The woman is given a mermaid's tail by the god of the sea. But the sailor then asks the sea god to give the woman legs and she learns to walk again.

The holiday period concludes with couples in unity, Gwen and Jim embracing and Roy kissing Coral as she runs shells through her fingers. The play ends at the beginning of the next school year: Miss Latrobe has taken her students outside to read Shakespeare's *King Lear*. Tom is asked to read Lear's opening speech, beginning 'Meantime we shall express our darker purpose', and these lines close the play.

Character summaries

Tom

A high-school student who is good at acting. He has terminal cancer but doesn't want his parents to worry about him. He is fond of Meg.

Harry

Harry is from Nottinghamshire in England and is married to Vic. He is the father of Tom, who has been diagnosed with cancer.

Vic

Vic is married to Harry. They are migrants from England. Tom is their son. She shows strength of character when Tom develops cancer.

Meg

Meg is a high-school student who is strong-willed and does not get on with her mother, Gwen. Meg is fond of Tom.

Gwen

Gwen is married to Jim and does not connect with her daughter, Meg. She nags her husband. Gwen is insecure and materialistic.

Jim

Jim is the husband of Gwen and the father of Meg. He seems submissive and passive but he is a good mediator.

Roy

Roy is the school principal and is married to Coral. Their son was killed in Vietnam. Roy seems overly concerned with his reputation.

Coral

Coral is married to Roy. She cannot accept the death of her son and has had an emotional breakdown.

BACKGROUND & CONTEXT

Historical, social and cultural contexts

Away centres on three Australian families and their Christmas holiday in 1967. The play uses its beach holiday setting, and the notion of going 'away', as a metaphor to explore its themes around a 'historical pivot point' or a time of great social and historical change. Set in the late 1960s, the play explores social and attitudinal divisions in the context of the iconic Australian summer beach holiday through juxtaposing the affluence, conservatism and less-open attitudes of Australia in the 1950s and early 1960s with the more radical and revolutionary attitudes of the late 1960s and early 1970s.

The 1960s

The period in which the play is set was a time of crucial change and transformation in Australia's historical, political, social and cultural identity. The inward-looking, largely Eurocentric and anti-Asian attitudes of the immediate post–World War II era in Australia were about to be challenged by a counterculture characterised by protest movements and a wave of Asian immigration which would change the face of Australia for years to come.

Australia reintroduced the ballot system or 'Draft' for selecting young men to go to fight in Vietnam in 1964 and, soon after, Australian Prime Minister Harold Holt announced that Australia would go 'all the way with LBJ' (US President Lyndon B Johnson). This saw Australia's commitment of troops to the Vietnam War rise to over 5000 by the mid-1960s. In the ten years from 1962 until 1972, during which Australia was involved in the Vietnam War, 60,000 troops were deployed, over 500 men were killed and several thousand were injured physically and/or psychologically.

The Vietnam War is called by some historians 'the Television War' or 'the Living Room War', since the proliferation of television ownership in the early 1960s meant that most Australian households saw the war unfold on the television news every evening. Families were faced nightly with up-to-date disturbing and cruel images and the ugly reality of war; suffering and death were beamed directly into people's homes.

The setting of *Away* in 1967 is crucial because 1966 had seen Australia suffer one of its worst defeats in Vietnam at the Battle of Long Tan, and public perceptions of the Vietnam War had reached a 'tipping point'.

In this context, *Away* can be seen to show the journey of the older conservative Australia of the early 1960s to the new identity and ideals that characterised Australia in the late 1960s and early 1970s. This new identity would blossom by 1970 with the first large anti–Vietnam War moratorium marches, the 1973 Nimbin Aquarius Festival and the steady stream of Vietnamese refugees or 'boat people' from 1975 through to the 1980s. In this sense, *Away* being set in 1967 means that it takes place at a time of great change, which allows Gow's play to comment on the nature of social change, whether it be the 1960s, the 1980s when the play was written, or even today.

Other historical and social references are scattered throughout the play, giving the audience insight into the period and the attitude of the characters in the play. Gwen frequently says she needs to 'take a Bex' (a 1960s medicinal powder taken mostly by women, which contained aspirin and caffeine), and references are made throughout the play to film actors of the era, such as Kim Novak, and also actors from earlier periods, including Laurence Olivier and Chips Rafferty.

The 1980s

Historically, politically and socially, the mid-1980s, when the play was written, were also times of great change in Australia. The election of the Bob Hawke government in 1983 was seen by many as a time of greater freedom after the austerity of the late 1970s and early 1980s. The perception of more open government, the floating of the Australian dollar, the deregulation of the Australian financial system, a drop in unemployment rates and a high volume of Asian immigration gave Australia a sense of openness, optimism and youthful exuberance.

Shakespearean allusions

Culturally, the play references Shakespeare, opening with a school production of *A Midsummer Night's Dream* and ending with a class reading of *King Lear*. In some ways the Shakespearean references can be seen as representations of the cultural and social shift from an Australia filled with the dreams and hopes of the early 1970s to a more polarised nation from 1975 to the early 1980s, which had to face the sacking of Prime Minister Gough Whitlam, rising unemployment figures and the arrival of Vietnamese immigrants by boat. In turn, the arrival of these immigrants forced Australia to confront the atrocities of the Vietnam War, as well as racism and other serious social divisions.

In *A Midsummer Night's Dream*, the characters pass through a period of bewilderment and disorientation to arrive at an acceptance of themselves and their loved ones, which is also to some extent the story of *Away*. In *King Lear*, on the other hand, Lear decides to divide his wealth among his own daughters, and the ensuing complications force all the characters to confront realities and their tragic consequences in much more disturbing ways. The referencing of *King Lear* at the conclusion of *Away* thus gives it a much darker ending than Puck's speech at the conclusion of *Midsummer Night's Dream* (the speech that opens *Away*), and points to Gow's fundamentally serious purpose in writing the play.

In all the above ways, *Away* is able to draw on multiple historical, social and cultural contexts while showing a world on the cusp of irreversible change. *Away* questions the nature of change and how events and circumstances change us as individuals, families and a larger community.

The playwright's historical context

Gow has often commented that he didn't get on with children of his own age when he was at school and that he instead frequently associated with kids about five years older than himself. This means that, in one sense, Tom can be seen as not so much reflecting Gow himself but as being a representation of the type of people and attitudes that Gow was drawn to as a young person:

> Because I was an only child I was already on my way to being a writer because I spent so much time observing everything. I found older kids more interesting because they were facing the call-up of the Draft and the expectations on them were enormous ... (Gow, cited in Bramwell 2006)

Also it is pertinent to note that, while at school, Michael Gow lost his older best friend David to leukaemia.

By 1970, Gow had joined the Australian Theatre for Young People and was acting in and writing plays, honing his skills as an actor and playwright. At Sydney University in 1973, he became involved primarily as an actor with SUDS (the Sydney University Dramatic Society), where he met his lifelong friend and artistic compatriot, director Neil Armfield. The late 1970s and early 1980s saw Gow's career as a professional actor blossom; and his love of Shakespeare, who also started his theatre career as an actor, is not without resonance.

In the mid-1980s Gow was on the cusp of many changes in his own life and he was also aware of the historical changes around him. He increasingly started to see himself as a writer rather than an actor and began to wonder about the points of change in people's lives as well as the agents for such change. He reflected on the mixed fates of people around him, some of whom had made their fortunes in finance and others who had suffered misfortune, relationship breakdowns and divorces. Although he had explored some aspects of this dislocation and social alienation in the highly successful play *The Kid* in 1983, it was not until Gow was asked in September 1985 if he could write a full-length play to premiere at the Griffin Theatre in January 1986 that he began in earnest to write *Away*.

As he wrote quickly to meet an early December deadline, Gow drew on his feelings about turning thirty and ageing, his childhood memories, his family and his memories of the 1960s, and his realisation of the horror of the growing conflict in Vietnam. The play also addresses Gow's perception of society's sense of hope and anticipation of change during the 1970s, as well as his resentment of the affluence, boredom and small-mindedness of the suburbs. Gow also stated at the time that he wanted to create a play that spoke particularly to young Australians about suffering, regeneration and hope.

Performance context

Away opened on 7 January 1986 at the Griffin Theatre Company's intimate Stables Theatre in Sydney, directed by Peter Kingston, in front of a capacity audience of 120 people. No-one, let alone the thirty-one-year-old Michael Gow, could know the impact the play would have. The short season at the Stables was a sellout and the production transferred to the Sydney Theatre Company's new Wharf Theatre, where it played to larger packed houses, collecting awards and accolades along the way, including a Green Room Award, the New South Wales Premier's Award for Best Play, the Sydney Theatre Critics Circle Award and an Australian Writer's Guild 'AWGIE' Award. Other productions were soon mounted by major theatre companies throughout Australia and by 1989 it was set as a secondary-school text. At last count it was one of the few Australian plays to have sold over 100,000 copies. *Away* was first performed overseas in the early 1990s and it is probably the most performed Australian play of all time.

In 1992, Michael Gow finally got the chance to direct *Away* and he changed the ending. Tom's role in the play finished on the beach, while Gow gave the reading of the extract from *King Lear* at the end of the play to Meg, suggesting the death of Tom after the summer beach holiday of 1967. Many criticised Gow for changing the ending and in response he said:

> Everyone says that *Away* is so much fun and so enjoyable. I think of it as a play about death. So I want to make this (1992) production mine and remind us of the darkness and

malevolence. The performance history of the play is of school and amateur productions and I feel it is my duty to stand up for the other side of the coin ... Even the fairies are not the little gumnut characters of some earlier versions ... These fairies are bad, and they have so much fun destroying Gwen's caravan in the storm. That's what it should be ... (cited in Bramwell 2006)

GENRE, STRUCTURE & LANGUAGE

Genre

Away is difficult to categorise into one genre and some critics have called it a hybrid play since it combines elements of comedy, tragedy, satire and magic realism.

On one level it is influenced by Gow's love of Shakespeare and is often broadly categorised as a **tragicomedy**. The play starts with Tom revealing his feelings for Meg and thus could be considered to be following the pattern of Shakespeare's comedies. Meg's parents' resistance to her relationship with Tom echoes the family objections to love represented in Shakespeare's *A Midsummer Night's Dream*. The play takes a darker turn when it is mentioned that the son of Roy (the principal of Tom and Meg's school) and Coral recently died in the Vietnam War. We are also given early hints of some darker tragedy surrounding Tom. The progression to the revelation of Tom's serious illness follows the classic pattern of a dramatic revelation in tragedy.

Key point

What makes *Away* particularly interesting is the way it combines stylistic elements from classical and Shakespearean tragedy and comedy with stylistic elements from other genres, including magic realism.

Social satire is also evident in the way *Away* comically paints a portrait of people from different social backgrounds and their interactions. Gwen's snobbery and Coral's encounters with strangers, such as Rick, give the play satirical undertones. In this sense the play can stylistically also be seen as a satire on the false pretensions of Australia's middle class.

While the sense of oppositional social and natural forces flows through the comedy, tragedy and satire of *Away*, the sense of transformative wonder is created in the play through the use of **magic realism**. Shakespeare's characters go 'away' into the forest but Gow's characters go to the beach to undergo transformation. The entrance of the Fairies to create the storm, along with the appearance of a mysterious woman (later identified as Coral) in a kaftan and the performance of the symbolic playlet, all give the play stylistic elements of magic realism. This narrative genre is usually characterised by fantastical elements or fantastical events occurring in a real-world setting, which serve to add a heightened sense of mystery or intensity. Gow uses the stylistic elements of magic realism at the climax of the play when the Fairies stage a 'spectacular storm' and just before Tom's cancer is revealed, to add dramatic emphasis to the play.

Structure

Away follows the traditional dramatic and narrative structure of a five-act drama while using the modern dramatic convention of interweaving or cutting between the stories and backgrounds of three families. In this sense the play breaks the classical dramatic principles of unity of time and place. The pattern of a five-act structure traditionally begins in Act One when the characters are established and the premise or setting is laid out. In *Away*, this cleverly happens in the context of the aftermath of a school production of Shakespeare's *A Midsummer Night's Dream*, contrasting the beginning of one story with the ending of another.

In Act Two of the five-act dramatic structure, problems or conflicts are revealed. In *Away* the revelation of these problems is not always overt. We learn that Tom has been in the hospital and that his father Harry feels that Tom might be embarrassed by them not having a 'flash' holiday and only going camping. These revelations run parallel to those of Meg's family, where we see that Meg hates her mother's control over her whole family's life and considers this to be hypocritical since Meg has heard that her mother left home at the age of eighteen. The problems and tragedy of Coral's and Roy's lives – including the loss of their son – are also woven into the fabric of Act Two.

Structurally, Act Three of *Away* reveals the *epitasis*: the intensification or stretching towards major events or a climax. This is often known as the dramatic structural point of **rising action**. Act Three starts on Christmas Eve with Coral talking to strangers and meeting Rick, a young man who is like the son she lost. Then we switch to a caravan city where Meg finally confronts Gwen about her over controlling and deceptive manner. This sequence of events is framed by the Campers appearing almost like a Greek chorus, voicing their concerns and grievances, and then a return to Coral and Rick. Finally the rising action of the play moves towards the storm and the appearance of the Fairies, who wreak havoc. Act Three ends after the storm, with Tom and his family celebrating small but precious joys.

The dramatic structure of the play then moves onto the **falling action**, which structurally works in opposition to the rising action and marks the narrative point where unknown details and plot twists are revealed. Act Four of *Away* sees Jim, Gwen and Meg ending up at the beach where Vic, Harry and Tom are staying. Harry reveals that Tom has cancer and the act ends with the performance of a symbolic play and a bonfire on the beach.

The final structural part of the play is the Act Five **denouement** and **resolution**: the holidays have ended and Tom is asked to read to his class from Shakespeare's *King Lear*. The play ends with couples and families in unity but with Tom, like Lear, preparing for his 'unburden'd crawl toward death'. The fact that Tom utters this speech in natural light, outside 'under the trees' implies catharsis and hope not only for him but also for the other characters who have taken the journey 'away'.

Some people also consider the five-act structure of *Away* to be cyclic or even open-ended, since the play starts with words from the end of Shakespeare's *A Midsummer Night's Dream* and ends with a speech from near the beginning of *King Lear*. Viewing the structure of the play from this perspective suggests that the journeys represented in the play are continuous and eternal; in other words, Tom's journey started before the play began and has not finished at the end of the play.

Language

Gow uses a range of language forms in *Away*. The play starts with the lyrical verse and rhyming couplets of Puck's closing speech from *A Midsummer Night's Dream*, delivered by Tom in the high-school play. The use of this verse not only serves as an allusion to Shakespeare's 'dream play' but ironically starts the play with a lyrical theatrical apology. The use of lyric verse is also replicated at the end of the play when Tom reads King Lear's first speech, and this allusion has more tragic undertones suggestive of or foreshadowing Tom's inevitable death.

These speeches and their lyrical language and tone can be firmly contrasted with the everyday, more colloquial speech used by most of the characters. The use of slang and colloquialisms provides an Australian cultural anchor point for the play, with words such as 'pressies', 'dunny' and 'Bex'. This informal style contrasts with more serious and formal language evident later in the play. Roy's informal initial speech serves to establish the setting, time and characters. His use of contractions sets up a familiarity with the audience, while his comparisons of the students' acting to 'a lot of little Chips Rafferties' (p.3) serves to firmly place his attitudes in a time which predates the 1967 setting of the play.

The length and verbosity of Roy's opening speech contrasts with the shorter utterances in the dialogue between Tom and Meg that follows. Here, colloquial speech not only makes these characters more believable, helping the audience relate to them more, but also serves to amplify the awkwardness of their affection for one another. This use of short lines of dialogue is also replicated in the conversation between Tom and his father Harry, when Tom arrives back late after walking home. Here, once again, the awkwardness of a relationship is reflected in short, staccato dialogue which increases the emotional intensity of the scene, since their brief lines belie complex, unspoken feelings.

The indirectness and awkwardness of Tom and Meg's initial dialogue is in stark contrast to the language used by Coral, whose first words are directed to the audience in a monologue, in which she reveals her emotional reaction to the performance of *A Midsummer Night's Dream*. The style and tone of this speech occurs nowhere else in the play.

Meg's father Jim uses reflective narrative tones when he describes to Meg the poverty in which he and Gwen used to live. Later in the play he tells of his first date with Gwen, and the reflective quality becomes more nostalgic. This encourages the audience identify more with Jim while also feeling more sympathetic towards Gwen despite her uptight and controlling nature.

The choral quality of some of the dialogue in the Camper sequence (Act Three, Scene Two) serves to give what could be an everyday conversation the non-naturalistic quality of a Greek chorus. The complaints of the Campers thus seem ironic and representative of the prejudices of small-minded Australians. The use of this choric language serves to make the Campers mouthpieces for the views of many Australians in the 1960s.

It is the absence of language that underscores the penultimate scene when, in Act Five, Scene One, Gow brings resolution and reconciliation to two of the three families involved in the plotline, through action and gestures.

SCENE-BY-SCENE ANALYSIS

Act One, Scene One – The school play (pp.3–4)

Summary: *The play opens as a school performance of Shakespeare's* A Midsummer Night's Dream *is coming to a close. Tom performs Puck's final speech of the play. Roy, the school's principal, commends the performances of the students, thanks helpers and thanks the parents for coming.*

Away opens with the lyric rhyming couplets of Puck's last speech in *A Midsummer Night's Dream* which emphasises one of the major themes of the play: making amends and seeking reconciliation. This speech is followed by Roy, the principal, whose thankyou speech contains cultural references which are signifiers of the 1967 cultural and social context of the play. Roy's patronising attitude and his inability to pronounce a Greek surname allude to the male Anglocentric nature of the Australian society and attitudes he represents.

Q What effect does Gow create by starting his play with Tom performing Puck's last speech from Shakespeare's *A Midsummer Night's Dream*?

Q How are some of the social and cultural attitudes of Australians in 1967 revealed in Roy's speech after the school play?

Act One, Scene Two – Backstage after the play (pp.4–11)

Summary: *Backstage after the show, Tom gives Meg a brooch. Gwen and Jim, Roy and Coral then Harry and Vic enter. They all talk about where they are going for Christmas and the summer holidays.*

When Tom utters the opening lines of this scene, 'You going away tomorrow?' he introduces one of central metaphors of the whole play, the summer holiday and the concept of going away to a different place to give a different perspective on relationships and the problems of life. This line will be given greater gravity later in the play when we find out that Tom has cancer: it may refer to a more permanent kind of departure and foreshadow Tom's inevitable death (which does not occur in this version of the play).

The dialogue between Tom and Meg is fast-paced and riddled with colloquial language. Tom even shows some bravado in this interchange when he mentions that he should have got Meg a 'bottle of gin'. All this serves to give a sense of adolescent awkwardness to the scene. Meg states in relation to Tom, 'Still waters run deep'. Tom's response that 'still waters stink' is comic but ironic in terms of one of the thematic preoccupations of the play: that stillness can bring stagnancy.

This exchange is interrupted by Gwen and Jim arriving. We get a sense of Gwen as bossy, over-reactive and discontented when she criticises the play. Then Roy and Coral enter. Roy's patronising tone and verbosity can be contrasted with his wife Coral's silence: when asked if she enjoyed the play, she '*looks away*' and '*doesn't respond*'. This reaction gives some indication of Coral's emotional and psychological state but her silence also creates an instant connection in the audience's mind between her and Tom, due to the earlier reference to him being 'quiet' and 'soulful'.

The joyful entrance of Tom's parents, Harry and Vic, completes the introduction of all the characters who will take the audience on a journey 'away'. Harry's comparison of his son's performance to the great English actor Laurence Olivier contrasts with Roy's earlier, more parochial references to the Australian actor Chips Rafferty. The reference to Olivier hints at Harry's English heritage and also clearly defines him and Vic as English immigrants who think outside of the constraints of the Australian cultural context.

When the discussion turns to the upcoming summer holidays, social divisions and snobbery emerge. It is revealed that Roy and Coral are flying to the Gold Coast while Gwen brags about going off in their new caravan – signalling her snobbery and a materialistic sense of identity. The fact that Tom, Harry and Vic are holidaying in a small lean-to tent evokes disdain and condescension from Gwen. The exit of Roy and Coral elicits a comment from Gwen about the tragedy of Roy and Coral's son, and Harry and Vic's exit brings out her snobbery about them *both* working in a factory. This indicates her contempt for the type of work Tom's parents are involved in and also exhibits a snobbery in Australia in general that was particularly strong in the 1950s and 1960s: a view that looked down on families in which the wife 'had' to work. Gwen even comments that 'they shouldn't be going away on a holiday if they can't afford one' (p.11). Tom overhears this conversation and defends his family by verbally attacking Gwen and hoping that she and her family have a 'rotten holiday'.

Key point

This sequence is one of the few where all the main characters of the play are on stage together. It is also significant that what reveals social divisions is the discussion about going away and the summer holiday.

Act One, Scene Three – Outside the school hall (p.12)

Summary: *Coral's soliloquy indicates that she has been moved by the performance; Roy is embarrassed by Coral's behaviour and wants to get her home.*

Coral's strange silence is broken with a soliloquy in which she identifies Tom with her lost son and expresses her desire to wake up like the female character (Titania) in the play she has just seen. This speech has a sense of foreshadowing since Coral longs for transformation, which she achieves later in the play. She also alludes to Tom's illness by stating that, 'he looked so sick yet wonderful, so white, so cold and burning' (p.12).

Q Why does Gow choose to make Coral's first utterances a soliloquy to the audience?

Q What is the effect of having Coral use such vivid and poetic language in her descriptions?

Act Two, Scene One – Later that night at Tom's home (pp.13–15)

Summary: *Tom arrives home; Harry is waiting up for him. Harry reminds Tom how important this holiday trip is for Tom's mother.*

When Tom arrives after walking home, his father is waiting up for him and his mother has already gone to bed. Harry is shown to be a caring father and husband because, although he makes excuses for why he stayed up, the audience can see it is because he is concerned for Tom's health. Both father and son try to placate one another but this only serves to create tension and awkwardness between the two.

Q How does Gow create interest and tension in this scene through what is unsaid as well as what is said?

Act Two, Scene Two – Late night at Meg's home (pp.15–19)

Summary: *At Meg's home, the family is all still up as Gwen is organising everyone with final packing for the holiday. Meg reluctantly helps but wants her mother to stop nagging and to go to bed. When Gwen does eventually go, Meg's father talks to her about Tom and reveals his worries that she might be pulled away from her family. He asks Meg to try to be more patient with her mother.*

Like the previous scene at Tom's house, this late-night scene at Meg's home is filled with tension. Gwen's repetitive nagging and negativity are made ironic because she believes that she is doing it all for her family. It is interesting to note that Meg stands up to Gwen while Jim does not. A box which is still to be put in the car becomes a point of contention. As a plot device, this event foreshadows later conflict and will take on greater significance when Jim's Christmas presents cannot be found.

When Gwen goes to bed, father and daughter talk and Jim expresses his concern that Meg might be 'drawn away' from their family. When Meg reminds him that her mother left home at eighteen or nineteen, Jim explains that Gwen's attachment to having plans and sticking to them is what got them through the tough conditions of the Great Depression and is what should carry them through the future. Meg reinforces her argument that people should not give into others 'for the sake of peace and quiet' (p.18).

Q Jim's story of coming through the Great Depression with Gwen gives us some insight into Gwen and her motivations. How does this story influence the audience's attitude towards Gwen?

Q How does Gow establish a connection between Meg and her father, and what is the dramatic function of this connection?

Act Two, Scene Three – Late night at Roy and Coral's home (pp.19–21)

Summary: *At Roy and Coral's house, Roy criticises Coral for her antisocial behaviour and points out how it undermines his position. He reminds Coral that they are not the only ones who have lost a son in war.*

In this scene the third family in the play, Roy and Coral, is explored, but with greater intensity and without the constraint used in the preceding scenes featuring Tom's and Meg's families. The reason behind Coral's behaviour is finally fully revealed. What is striking in this scene is the difference between the reactions of Roy and of Coral to the death of their son in Vietnam.

Roy is unable to express his feelings about the loss of his son; he finds some solace in his social position and in social platitudes and idioms such as 'we are not the first people in the history of the world to lose a son in war' (p.20), and the belief that there comes a time when grief must end. He labels Coral's behaviour as weird and selfish. He is unable to cope with her emotional expressions of grief. Coral, on the other hand, has let her grief consume her; she is unable to move forward and lives in the past. Her repeated references to Kim Novak, a famous Hollywood actress of the 1950s and 1960s, signify her desire to re-create her relationship with Roy, and to recapture something of the past.

This scene shows the gulf between the pair and the sense of reconciliation at the end of the scene seems tentative, due to the trauma and grief that lie just below the surface.

Q How are Roy's and Coral's reactions to their son's death indicative of their personalities and attitudes?

Q Does Roy's use of platitudes and idioms encourage an audience to sympathise with him less than they might sympathise with Coral? Explain your answer.

Act Two, Scene Four – Much later the same night at Tom's home (pp.21–2)

Summary: *Vic, who has been unable to sleep, has left her bed because she heard a noise; Tom says he got up because he was thirsty. The two talk and Vic apologises in advance for the holiday not being 'flash' and for not being able to afford to give Tom much in the way of Christmas presents. Vic asks Tom to pretend to enjoy the holiday to please his father.*

The genuine expression of care and affection between Tom and his mother can be directly contrasted with the exchanges between Coral and Roy and between Meg and her mother. The scene ironically mirrors the scene between Tom and his father, since Vic asks Tom to try to look as if he is having a good time on the holiday to please his father, just as Harry had asked Tom to pretend for Vic's sake. This helps the audience understand not just the genuine affection Tom's parents hold for him, but also the way in which they care for each other.

Key point

This scene provides a counterpoint to the scene before, since what threatens to take away Tom's family's happiness is not wholly revealed.

Act Three, Scene One – Coral and Roy at a Gold Coast hotel (pp.23–8)

Summary: *At a Gold Coast hotel, Coral meets a woman and then a newly married young man called Rick. Roy arrives looking for Coral. Rick decides to wait for his wife.*

Coral attempts to consciously connect to other people more but her social skills are awkward at best. She converses initially with a woman called Leonie and her efforts at normality distress Leonie, until Leonie eventually reveals that her own husband is having an affair with a young woman. It is almost comical, and also moving, that Coral's unhappiness draws out the problems and distress of others.

When Leonie leaves, Coral starts talking to a newlywed called Rick; again she draws the misery out of others as Rick reveals that he has married a girl he 'likes' rather than 'loves'. He married to avoid going to Vietnam and Coral's reply to this news, 'marriage or the jungle' (p.27), is a kind of black humour. Her statement that Rick would have made a 'good soldier' draws a direct parallel between Rick and her dead son.

Q Why does Coral continue to talk to Leonie even though it is obvious that Leonie wants to leave?

Q What parallels might an audience draw between Coral's dead son and Rick?

Act Three, Scene Two – A tent and caravan city (pp.28–37)

Summary: *Gwen's family is at a holiday place filled with caravans; Jim is looking for a cardboard box in which he put Gwen's Christmas present. Gwen eventually admits that she deliberately left the box behind. She leaves. A group of campers asks Jim to sign a petition.*

Gwen's confrontations with Meg take on an almost comic absurdity in this scene. By consciously leaving Jim's box of presents behind, Gwen is trying to reinforce her belief that, without her systems and controls, the family would not cope. When Meg exposes what her mother has done, it is Jim who – despite being the one most affected by Gwen's actions – acts as the mediating force between Gwen and Meg.

With Gwen's exit, the tone of the scene changes. Jim tells a tale which is both nostalgic and didactic, about when he first courted Gwen and took her to see the film *Gone with the Wind*. The story draws a parallel between the forthright power of Vivien Leigh's character (Scarlett O'Hara) to survive and thrive, and Gwen's domineering resilience. Through telling this story, Jim not only generates some sympathy for and understanding of Gwen, but he also sets himself up as someone who is philosophical and sits outside of the world of the play, contextualising and making sense of the people and situations the audience is witnessing.

The arrival of the Campers shifts the pace and tone of the scene once more. Even though they have come 'away' for the holidays, they bring their petty concerns, prejudices and conformity with them from the world they have left behind. The non-naturalistic Greek-chorus quality of the Campers makes this scene a poignant satire of conservative suburban Australia. The end of the scene is punctuated by Jim and Meg telling funny nostalgic anecdotes of previous holidays. Jim's act of tearing up the Campers' petition is both symbolic and cathartic.

Q What is the dramatic function of the placement of the Campers' petition sequence straight after Gwen and Meg's argument and Jim's anecdote about Gwen and *Gone with the Wind*?

Q How does Jim's story about Gwen and the film *Gone with the Wind* help an audience understand Gwen better?

Act Three, Scene Three – New Year's Eve (pp.37–40)

Summary: *On New Year's Eve, Coral meets Rick again up on the roof of the hotel. They talk intimately and Rick tells Coral that his wife, Susie, is jealous of him spending time with her. Roy arrives on the roof, looking for Coral. Rick leaves. The scene ends with Roy threatening to arrange shock treatment for Coral and lock her up. Coral calmly tells Roy not to worry about her, takes the room key and leaves to weigh things up and come to a decision.*

The scene has sexual undertones, with Coral sneaking off with Rick to the rooftop, but this serves to explore more complex themes. Rick, who escaped conscription by getting married, now does not want to accept the societal expectations he feels pressured by. By the same token, Coral sees Rick as a substitute for her son and this sequence shows her inability to escape the past.

When Roy discovers Coral and Rick together he is taken aback and angry, while Coral acts as if they are all together as a family, with Rick as the son they lost. When Roy sends Rick away, he threatens to take Coral to a doctor for electroconvulsive therapy and then to lock her up (presumably in an institution). The audience sympathises with Coral at this point, since we realise that she seeks from strangers the comfort and understanding that her husband denies her.

Coral in this scene has parallels with another character made famous by Vivien Leigh, Blanche DuBois in *A Streetcar Named Desire*. Like Coral, Blanche has experienced a tragic loss and subsequently struggles to maintain a secure grasp on reality, and to engage positively with those close to her. Blanche's famous line from the end of the play, 'I have always depended on the kindness of strangers', has a faint echo in Coral's sense of alienation and her desire to form a new (and improbable) bond with Rick.

The calmness with which Coral reacts to Roy's threats is both pathetic and strange, giving the audience a sense of anticipation of the fate that awaits her.

Q How does this scene act as a catalyst for bringing both Coral and Roy to a climactic point which allows them to change?

Q What makes Roy feel so desperate that he threatens Coral with institutionalisation and 'shock treatment'?

Act Three, Scene Four – Storm scene (pp.40–1)

Summary: *Fairies enter and stage a storm sequence. Jim and Gwen pack up everything and the Fairies and the storm wreak havoc.*

The reappearance of the Fairies from the final scene of *A Midsummer Night's Dream* (performed at the beginning of the play) gives this pivotal point in *Away* the stylistic feel of magic realism. The emotional turmoil of the previous scenes is symbolically brought to a climax in the storm, which combines the real (Jim and Gwen trying to pack up and save material objects from the storm) with the surreal (the Fairies creating a storm to the sound of Mendelssohn's 'Wedding March'). The storm symbolically forces the characters in the play to confront their petty arguments, concerns and attachment to objects by nature confronting them.

Q What is the dramatic function of this scene being staged in a different style to the scenes around it?

Act Three, Scene Five – Tom, Vic and Harry avoid the storm (p.41)

Summary: *Tom, Vic and Harry gather on a beach just after a storm. They are happy with the simple Christmas presents they have given one another.*

Unlike Meg's family and Roy and Coral, Tom and his family have not had to face the 'storm' and they remain calm, happy and content. They have not ended up dislocated and physically displaced like Meg's family, perhaps due to their non-attachment to material objects. On another level, they have not had to suffer the emotional and psychological breakdown that is evident in Coral and her relationship with Roy. This holiday 'away' has strengthened relationships between members of Tom's family and they find happiness in Christmas.

Key point

The sound and lighting descriptions at the beginning of this scene, along with the costume descriptions, are very detailed and specific and give some sense of the mood and atmosphere that Gow wants directors to create here.

Act Four, Scene One – Jim and Gwen meet Harry and Vic (pp.42–7)

Summary: *The storm has made Jim, Gwen and Meg leave their caravan site and they have ended up at the beach where Vic, Harry and Tom are staying. While Vic and Harry talk about the virtues of the place, they see a woman in a kaftan. When Vic takes Gwen for a walk, Harry talks to Jim and reveals to him that Tom has terminal cancer and is in remission. Vic and Gwen return and Vic invites Gwen and Jim to the Campers' amateur night.*

The storm has brought the turmoil of Jim, Gwen and Meg's world to the fore and the 'natural' world (as represented by the storm and the beach) has overcome the human world of emotions and materialism. Meg's natural instincts or intuition have brought her family to the same place as Tom's family. Even Gwen, now stripped of material objects, must embrace change. She initially resists this and launches into a tirade about mad people and those with no direction or ambition. When Vic takes her for a walk, Gwen seems to come back a changed woman. We never hear what happened or what Vic said to her. As an audience, we guess that Vic has told Gwen what Harry tells Jim: that Tom has terminal cancer and, although he is in remission, his leukaemia will eventually return.

In this major turning point of the play, Gwen undergoes a transformation, just like the characters in Shakespeare's *A Midsummer Night's Dream*. After Vic and Harry leave, Gwen presumably has realised that she has tried to control too many things and people in her life.

She embraces feelings and nature: this is represented by her asking Jim to come down to the water with her.

Q Why do you think Harry and Vic decide to tell Jim and Gwen about Tom's cancer?

Act Four, Scene Two – Tom and Meg on the beach (pp.47–52)

Summary: *When Tom and Meg walk together on the beach, Tom reveals that he knows the strange 'artistic' woman in the kaftan is Coral. He makes advances towards Meg and asks her to sleep with him, then tells her about his terminal illness. Meg gently rejects Tom's advances and they continue to be friends.*

Now that the storm and fate have brought Tom and Meg back together again, Tom pushes the sexual dimensions of their relationship by asking Meg to have sex with him. The dialogue between the two is clipped, stilted and awkward. The fact that Tom tells Meg about his terminal illness straight after making sexual advances emphasises the awkwardness and urgency of his request, which Meg gently rejects.

Despite the gravity and sensitivity of this moment of Tom's desperation, Gow is able to add lightness, eliciting humour when Meg tells Tom that he is too skinny, which prompts Tom to suggest he should do a Charles Atlas bodybuilding course, before he quickly does push-ups on the beach. (Charles Atlas was a circus strongman and bodybuilder whose popular exercise program was widely advertised in the 1940s to 1960s.)

When Coral enters the scene carrying wood for the bonfire, their connection or bond is obvious. Although both have death looming large in their lives, the potential to build a fire and act in the concert seem to fuel their love of life.

Q How is the awkwardness between Tom and Meg contrasted with the comfortable familiarity shown between Tom and Coral?

Q What is the dramatic function of bringing Tom and Meg back together during this scene?

Act Four, Scene Three – The amateur night concert (pp.52–5)

Summary: *At the Campers' amateur night, Tom and Coral perform a playlet about a sailor who dies and, as a ghost, falls in love with a woman who is given a mermaid's tail. But the sailor then asks the sea god to give the woman legs and she learns to walk again. When Tom and Coral exit, everyone notices a bonfire on the beach.*

This scene starts with an MC telling old hackneyed jokes. The vaudeville atmosphere is jovial and is topped off with the MC playing a ukulele. He then introduces Tom and Coral's playlet, which is entitled *The Stranger on the Shore*. The story they tell is a strange combination of 'The Flying Dutchman' and 'The Little Mermaid'. These stories are metaphoric representations of Tom's and Coral's worlds. For Tom this is symbolised in the death of the sailor; for Coral, her world and the death of her son are represented in a woman who has seen the person she loves pass on to another world.

The playlet reinforces the healing power of love, since it shows both a woman returned to normality by the power of love and a young man who, by accepting love, is able to accept his own fate. Both these characters have undergone a transformation which is now complete. The bonfire is symbolic of warmth, life and hope.

Q At the end of this scene, most people walk towards the fire; however, Vic and Harry '*leave the stage in another direction*'. Why do you think Gow has written this stage direction?

Act Five, Scene One – Mimed sequence showing returning home (p.56)

Summary: *Two families act out their return home. Jim finally gives Gwen her Christmas present. Coral gives Roy a hat full of shells.*

This scene is mimed or acted out without dialogue and marks the transition from the characters going 'away' on holiday and returning 'home'. Staging, music and lighting directions are important to this scene. Mendelssohn's 'Nocturne' music from his *A Midsummer Night's Dream Suite*, the split-scene staging and the bright, summery morning light at the end of the scene mark the mood change from the fantasy 'away' world to a 'home' which embraces enlightenment and change and symbolises a new day in a familiar but transformed place.

Jim's gift of slippers to Gwen and her acceptance of this gift symbolise comfort, familiarity, love and forgiveness. The removal of the cardboard carton by Meg represents the past being removed so that her family can move forward. Coral's gift to Roy – a hat full of shells – symbolises the power of nature and love and the renewal that nature, and the sea in particular, can bring. The appearance of Miss Latrobe at the end of the scene heralds a new day and a new school year.

Q Why does Gow use a scene without dialogue at this point in the play?

Act Five, Scene Two – The schoolyard (pp.56–7)

Summary: *It is a new school year and Miss Latrobe takes her students outside to read Shakespeare's* King Lear. *Tom is asked to read Lear's opening speech.*

This scene's full-circle return to Shakespeare gives a sense of completion, transformation and growth to the play as a whole. It is also significant that Gow, in his 1992 version, changed the final speech so that it is read by Meg; this would have suggested that Tom had died before the new school year began, giving the play a much more pessimistic ending.

The broader concerns and message of this scene and the end of the play remain. In this speech, Lear confronts the end of his life, thinking that he is bringing it to a harmonious close; but in fact he is only initiating a tragic chain of events.

The characters in the play have all had to confront issues of life, death and the nature of mortality and, after having been 'away' and transformed, they 'unburden'd crawl toward death'.

Q What is the significance of having Tom read King Lear's speech at the end of the play?

CHARACTERS & RELATIONSHIPS

Tom

Key quotes

'Still waters stink.' (p.7)

'I hope you have a rotten holiday.' (p.11)

'They don't know. That I know. They want me to think I'm going to be right as rain.' (p.50)

'You don't belong here. You must return to your own world …' (p.54)

'… while we / Unburden'd crawl toward death.' (p.57)

As the protagonist of *Away*, Tom is the central character who initiates changes in others. We initially see him portrayed as a budding young actor, a potential Chips Rafferty or Laurence Olivier. This characterisation of him – as someone who can harness the powers of the imagination and creativity – has deeper significance as the play unfolds since we see his ability to escape or at least cope with the tragic circumstances of his own life.

At the play's beginning, in the role of Puck in *A Midsummer Night's Dream*, Tom promises that he will 'restore amends' and this is exactly what he is able to do when he changes other characters throughout the play. He sees staying still as stagnancy, and transformation and change as necessary. In his relationships and interactions he embodies these beliefs by helping people grow and change. As himself, he is the son who transforms his parents. As Puck, he is director of the Fairies and forces of nature that push Gwen towards the circumstances that make her change. As the sailor in the playlet, he restores Coral to life and hope. Finally, as King Lear, he brings the audience to the point of tragedy and death, to help them realise that transformation and reconciliation can generate love and hope.

Tom is often caring and compassionate: traits demonstrated by his role in his family. Though his youth and illness might suggest vulnerability and the need for protection, in fact it is he who is protective of his parents. His desire to stand up for them is reflected in his wishing Gwen a 'rotten holiday' when he overhears her putting his family down. He also doesn't want his parents to know that he is fully aware of the state of his cancer.

Tom's other important relationship in the play is with Meg. Tom likes Meg and he fluctuates in his conversations with her from adolescent awkwardness to admiration to sardonic dark humour. His desperation and fear are evident when he makes a sexual advance towards her, but it is his humour that eventually prevails in this awkward encounter.

Key point

The audience relates to Tom straight away. He is set up from the beginning as being separate from the other characters, even his own family. He is both otherworldly and real and his awkwardness and humour can be seen to contrast and work with the wisdom and transformative power he shows in the play.

Meg

Key quotes

'Still waters run deep. My father's always saying that.' (p.7)

'I want to be certain like that.' (p.18)

'I don't think anyone should give in for the sake of peace and quiet. I don't.' (p.18)

'You knew what was in that box. You left it behind. I want to know why.' (p.32)

'I wanted us to take a chance for once and see what was here.' (p.48)

Meg is representative of youth and the desire for generational change that is explored by the play and its 1967 setting. She is strong-willed and opinionated, and has a desire for independence that is tied to her complex relationships with her parents. Ironically, she is fond of and connected to her father even though she resents his pliable nature. Conversely, Meg does not get on with her mother, Gwen. She is acutely aware of Gwen's snobbery and, on one level, her relationship with Tom can be seen as a revolt against Gwen.

Meg's constant challenging of her mother can be interpreted as representing the questioning by a younger emerging generation in 1967 of the attitudes and opinions of the older generation. When Gwen challenges her daughter and accuses her of not appreciating everything she has done for her, Meg accuses Gwen of selfishness. However, Meg's relationship with her family – and particularly with Gwen – is not just confrontational but also positive and healing at times. For example, after the storm it is Meg's natural instinct or intuition that brings her family to the same place as Tom's family, and this in turn helps to bring about Gwen's transformation and catharsis.

Although Meg has not moved away from home like her mother, she is able to lead her family to a new world and new perspective, symbolically indicated by her leading them on a transformational journey to a 'place' (both geographical and psychological) where Gwen's old attitudes must be replaced by a new outlook. In the generational conflict with her mother, Meg triumphs; her insistence on movement and change is represented by her final act of taking Gwen's burdens and the cardboard carton offstage near the end of the play.

Key point

Although Meg is shown to be open-minded, smart and accepting, it seems that these are qualities she displays to almost everyone except her mother, Gwen. If Tom is the most timeless character in the play, Meg seems to be the most real character and the one with whom the audience finds it easiest to identify.

Coral

Key quotes

'When that woman woke up and saw that donkey at her feet I thought my heart would break.' (p.12)

'Do you still think I look like Kim Novak?' (p.20)

'We won't mention helicopters, or jungles, or mines –' (p.20)

'I'll gather my thoughts and turn things over and over in my mind.' (p.40)

'How I yearn for the land, the sky, the grass, but to walk causes me terrible pain in my nether regions.' (p.54)

When we meet Coral at the beginning of the play, we can see that she has had an emotional breakdown, which we later learn is due to the death of her son in the Vietnam War. Her inability to accept her son's death has caused Coral to lose her social identity and she struggles to socially connect to people because she is lost for words.

Coral initially seems caught in her own grief, speaking primarily in mournful and overly emotional utterances. It is interesting to note that she easily establishes a connection with young men, as seen in her instant rapport with Rick and Tom; this is primarily because she sees her son in both these young men. Coral receives no sympathy or help from her husband Roy; she reacts in a childlike fashion to his demands and in return he treats her like a child.

When Coral attempts to socialise again, while on holiday, she latches onto a new acquaintance, Leonie. Coral's emotional state seems to draw distress out of Leonie, who wrenches herself free of Coral while revealing that her husband is having an affair with a younger woman. Coral then approaches Rick. She immediately relates to Rick as if he were her son. This could signify that Coral sees interacting with Rick as a way to keep her son imaginatively alive.

After her husband threatens her with shock treatment and institutionalisation, Coral turns up as the mysterious woman in a kaftan at the beach where Tom and his family are holidaying. This second meeting with Tom seems to bring about a healing process in Coral which reaches its catharsis in the playlet they perform and the bonfire on the beach. Her final action of pouring shells through her hands symbolises her acceptance of her son's death and mortality as a force of nature which must be acknowledged, not denied.

Key point

The two characters whose fate most concerns an audience are Tom and Coral. Coral's character undergoes great changes in the course of the play and she reaches resolution with herself, the death of her son and, finally, her husband.

Gwen

Key quotes

'They both work, don't they? In a factory isn't it? I'm sure that's what I heard. A lean-to. They shouldn't be going on a holiday if they can't afford one.' (p.11)

'No one asked them to come out to this country. They have no right to behave any differently.' (p.11)

'If we're going to have any sort of reasonable holiday we're going to have to pay for it.' (p.16)

'Throw your future away. Give it away. Throw what I have done, we have done, in our faces.' (p.32)

'Don't protect me. Tell me what I'm feeling.' (p.46)

Gwen is portrayed as a nagging housewife, a snob who is filled with prejudice and is too attached to material objects. She is overly controlling of her family and seems to have a complaint or opinion about almost everything. As the play progresses, we realise that her headaches and continuous taking of Bex powders are indications that she is not coping and that her need to control and her lack of acceptance have taken a great personal emotional toll, and a toll on her relationships.

Her lack of emotional connection to her daughter has resulted in Meg resenting her mother and even wishing her dead. Meg despises Gwen because she is always nagging, seems materialistic and is bossy and manipulative. Gwen's insecurity, represented in her obsession with materialism, can be seen to stem from the poverty of the Great Depression. This helps the audience to empathise with Gwen, and to understand that, while she is often unkind and insensitive towards her daughter, there are reasons for her behaviour and she is trapped in her own cycle of unhappiness.

At the end of the play, her husband Jim gets rid of her medication and Gwen allows her daughter to discard the material objects she is attached to. Her transformation is emotional and physical: her headaches and reliance on medication dissipate and are transformed after the storm.

It is interesting to note that it is Gwen who leads the thunderous applause for Coral and Tom at the end of their performance of *The Stranger on the Shore*. Soon after, she accepts the present of a pair of slippers from her husband, symbolising her new acceptance of comfort and, perhaps, domesticity. These significant changes in her personality represent the journey she has taken during the play, demonstrating how events and relationships have shifted her understanding of the world and her own behaviour.

Key point

Gwen starts off as almost a caricature of a stereotypical housewife of the 1960s but the storm and other events strip her of her attachment to objects and self-delusion. She eventually ends up as a very real character who must begin to acknowledge her own feelings.

Jim

Key quotes

'You might be drawn away, pulled away from us. That would be very upsetting.' (p.17)

'… her plans are the way we have to go … We have to support her, follow her, stick to her plans.' (p.18)

'My wife is not really an angry woman. She has high hopes.' (p.44)

Jim is, on one level, pliable and submissive to his wife and her demands and hopes. But on another level he signifies openness and normality. It is interesting to note that he is one of the few characters outside of Tom's family who does not change. His wife's obnoxious behaviour, the holiday, the arguments between his daughter and wife and even the storm, do not change him.

Jim does not need revelations or external forces to change him because he places his family first. By embracing Gwen at the end of the play, Jim is shown to be accepting of the changes Gwen has undergone and once again ready to share the journey his wife and family will take him on.

Vic

Key quotes

'But if you do get cheesed off … try and look like you're having a real ball.' (p.22)

'You can act, we all know that now. Maybe that's what you'll end up doing with yourself.' (p.22)

'The world is full of interesting people.' (p.43)

Vic is caring and thoughtful towards both her husband and her dying son. In some ways she is less overprotective than Harry: at the beginning of the play she tells Harry that Tom will be all right walking home. She seems to hold some hope that Tom will live for longer, since she makes at least one statement about his future. She has a loving husband and son and she treasures the time they spend together.

It is interesting that it is her character that is most communicative initially with Jim and Gwen when they arrive at the beach after the storm. She waxes lyrical about the virtues of the place. Her character is not just a contented optimist but also has a deep sense of place and history. It is ironic that it is Vic, the hard-working English immigrant whose son is dying, who is the first character in the play to express a strong connection to the Australian landscape and a sense of place.

Harry

Key quotes

'... if you could try and ... look like you're having a good time. I'm asking this for your mother.' (p.14)

'Our son is very sick. It's cancer of the blood. He was very bad this year, we thought it was time to get ready.' (p.45)

'We don't look back and we don't look forward.' (p.45)

As the father of a boy who is dying of cancer, Harry is unexpectedly gracious and thankful for the time he has with his son. He and Vic have come from England as post–World War II immigrants and are content with the life they found in Australia even though they live almost in working poverty.

Harry is caring and selfless. He has planned the simple holiday in a 'lean-to' tent for his wife and asks Tom to pretend he is having a good time, for Vic's sake. He does not live in the past, and nor does he live for the future; this means that he is representative of a person who has been confined to the present by tragedy but who accepts each day and opportunity as it comes.

When Harry tells Jim about Tom's illness it is not to elicit sympathy; he thinks that Jim may 'need' to know, since he suspects that Meg is fond of Tom and he feels it is his responsibility to tell her father about Tom's inevitable fate.

Roy

Key quotes

'I can't go on turning up at school functions with you if you're going to behave like a ghost.' (p.19)

'We are not the first people in the history of the world to lose a son in war.' (p.20)

'Do you want me to arrange shock treatment? I can. I looked into it.' (p.40)

Roy, the school principal, is married to Coral and cares more for his reputation than for his wife. He seems unable to face the death of his son and instead finds some comfort in his social position and social platitudes. By labelling Coral as weird and selfish, he distances himself from her and from their shared suffering; he does not choose to experience or face his grief, but rather to deny it.

He also seems obsessed with what other people think and with maintaining a certain material standard of living. These priorities dominate his existence to the point that they compromise his relationships and the wellbeing of those around him (particularly his wife). In this sense, we can see Roy as representative of the sterility of the 1950s and early 1960s, when an attachment to reputation and materialism actively blocked change and transformation.

Roy's threat to institutionalise Coral and give her shock treatment is the ultimate metaphor for his desire to lock up or eradicate his emotional and psychological worlds. Just as he refuses to engage with his feelings about the loss of his son, he wants to deny Coral the opportunity to connect with her own feelings. However, Roy's final action – burying his face in the seashells Coral holds, and kissing her hands – suggests that he too has the potential to change. The action is a silent and potent symbol of his repentance and transformation into a person who will embrace the reality of nature and of a world that moves forward, touched by events and people and the emotions they evoke.

Minor characters

Rick

Rick is a discontented, newly married young man with whom Coral connects while on holiday at a hotel on the Gold Coast. Coral sees her own dead son in him, although Rick doesn't seem to understand this (pp.26–7). His character reflects the life that Coral's son might have had if he had not gone to Vietnam and died.

In the second scene between Coral and Rick, we get the sense that he also might be on the cusp of a transformation since Coral has forced him to confront uncertainties in himself which he had never faced up to before (pp.38–9).

Leonie (the Woman)

Leonie is the first person with whom Coral tries to start a conversation during her holiday. She helps to exemplify the concept that 'normality' and happiness can often hide distress and discontent. Coral's attempts at normal conversation upset Leonie, shifting her out of her comfort zone.

When Leonie eventually reveals that her own husband is having an affair, we get the sense that she did not want to reveal or face this fact; when she immediately leaves Coral to go off to dinner (p.25), it is clear that Leonie would rather hide her distress than confront it. She can be seen to represent one potential avenue that is open to Coral: to hide her feelings of grief and to suffer in silence. In this way, Leonie echoes Roy and both characters provide contrasts with Coral, emphasising the significance of her emotional openness.

The Campers

The Campers function like a Greek chorus, voicing their concerns and grievances. The choral quality of their dialogue is non-naturalistic, indicating that their role is largely symbolic; they can be seen to represent the prejudices of narrow-minded Australians in the 1960s (pp.34–5). The trivial concerns and complaints of the Campers are those of the domestic suburban world from which they come. The dramatic function of their characters is to make a satirical comment on that world and on people who never want to leave the comfort of their own beliefs, prejudices and suburban existence when they go 'away'.

Key point

The Campers do not appear on stage with Gwen. Chorus-like, they echo the attitudes and values that Gwen seems to embrace. After they leave, Gwen enters, during the storm which changes her significantly. The way the Campers reflect her attitudes seems to foreshadow Gwen confronting and letting go of her old identity and values.

The Fairies

In the context of the play, the Fairies are not really a set of characters so much as an agent for change. They initially appear as characters in a performance of *A Midsummer Night's Dream* (p.3) and then are used as more symbolic representations of the forces of nature when they stage the storm, which influences events and brings about changes in the characters in the play (p.40).

In one sense, their second appearance can be seen to function like the stage convention in ancient Greek theatre called *deus ex machina*, a device whereby a person or object appears unexpectedly to provide an external or artificial force which drives the play to a conclusion or resolution.

THEMES, IDEAS & VALUES

Family

Key quotes

'Some people may be happy living like pigs but I'm not ... Unless you'd rather live like that?' (Gwen, p.11)

'We were very proud tonight. I glanced sideways at your mother at one point and her face was glowing, it was shining. She was very happy.' (Harry, p.14)

'And you are so important to your mother's plans.' (Jim, p.18)

'We are not the first people in the history of the world to lose a son in war ... That's what history is, people picking themselves up, pulling themselves together and going on.' (Roy, p.20)

'We don't look back and we don't look forward. We have this boy and we won't have him for long.' (Harry, p.45)

Away essentially follows the interaction and transformation of three families over the course of the summer holiday period in 1967. The play is about a physical and a metaphoric journey of these three families and the ideas and values they represent.

Meg's family represents a family at a crossroads; a family who always looks towards the future without acknowledging the past or the present. Gwen's plans and control over every member of her family are what has brought them to a position of comfort and middle-class affluence, but it is also her control, snobbery and attachment to material objects that her daughter Meg revolts against. Meg's parents fear losing her and it is only through being fundamentally transformed that their family will be saved.

On an allegorical level, the transformation of Meg's family in the play is representative of the fundamental changes in Australian values and attitudes regarding the notion of family in the late 1960s and the 1970s.

In this way, Gow is able to use events in the life of one fictional family to tell a story about the wider society.

Coral and Roy have lost their son in the Vietnam War and the changes they have to undergo as a family include having to reassess the way they relate to one another and the world. Coral lives psychologically and emotionally in the past, while Roy thinks he is moving forward but is relying on the ideas, clichés and values of the past. The play explicitly rejects the values of the immediate post–World War II era and the 1950s; the platitudes and idioms that Roy relies on are not enough. It is only later, when Roy and Coral accept the death of their son and reconnect with the present, that they are able to move forward as a couple.

In this sense, the play seems to be advocating acceptance of the values of the late 1960s and early 1970s, values which are consistent with individuals holding the view that they should live in the present, not in the past or the future. This has an added resonance when we consider that Gow wrote the play in the 1980s, when Australians were once more reassessing the values they should carry through to the future.

Tom's family acts as a counterpoint to all the other families in the play. If Meg and her parents represent families that lives for the future and Coral's family signifies those that live in the past, then Tom, Vic and Harry represent families that live in the present. They are immigrants from England and have given up their homeland and extended family for a life as a nuclear family unit in Australia. Vic and Harry love their new country but are preparing for the prospect of living in Australia in working poverty, with their son Tom no longer being part of their lives. They do not look back to the past; nor do they look to the future. Rather, they cherish the present and the moments they have with their son.

Tom and his parents can be seen to characterise the values of modern Australia, which came into focus in the late 1960s but resonated again in the 1980s and are still widely held today. These values include openness, tolerance, inclusiveness and optimism.

Key point

Each of the three families in the play is in crisis and must face some form of loss to achieve reconciliation.

Life and death

Key quotes

'Is it better for them to die like that? Looking like gods?' (Coral, p.12)

'We were picked out to pay ... We've paid. I can't bring him back.' (Roy, p.21)

'The world is full of mad people ... They're everywhere. Like ants, swarming everywhere, no direction, no ambition –' (Gwen, p.44)

'The Chinese don't believe in being too upset when someone dies. That would mean you thought they'd died too soon ...' (Harry, p.45)

'*... shake all cares and business from our age ... while we / Unburden'd crawl toward death.*' (Tom quoting King Lear, p.57)

It is not unintentional that the last word of *Away* is 'death'. Nor is it coincidental that the title of the play strongly suggests death, dying and loss. A powerful sense of death resonates throughout this play. The characters are confronted by death on two sides: from the past – as represented by the death of Coral and Roy's son in Vietnam – and from the future – through the looming, seemingly inevitable death of Tom.

As the father and mother of a boy who is dying of cancer, Harry and Vic are thankful for the time they have with their son. In this sense, although death can be seen to define Tom's family, it also gives them the opportunity to truly live and enjoy each moment with one another.

Conversely, the death of Coral and Roy's son has shaped their lives in negative ways. Roy lives in a world of denial while Coral lives a half-life in isolation from the world, dominated by her own emotions and her internal life. Coral and Roy are also influenced by the more positive qualities that Tom is able to share, despite his being so close to death.

Tom ultimately gives Coral the understanding and acknowledgement that draws her back to engage with the external world. Moreover, it is the news that Tom is dying of cancer that causes Gwen and her family to change and attempt to live together without the controls and trappings of materialism, snobbery and ambition.

Although death seems to define all the characters in *Away*, it is by accepting and acknowledging death that each family and each character is able to embrace life. Harry, Vic and Tom have already done this when the play begins and their simple holiday reinforces the extent to which they value life and live each moment for the joy it brings.

The mimed penultimate scene in Act Five, Scene One brings resolution and reconciliation to the other two families. We see Jim finally give Gwen the Christmas present he got for her and Coral offers Roy a handful of shells. Jim's gift of slippers to Gwen and her acceptance of this gift, along with Meg removing the cardboard box, symbolise Gwen embracing a life not dependent on materialism but characterised by comfort, familiarity, love and forgiveness. Coral's gift to Roy, a hat full of shells, symbolises them re-embracing their life together and acknowledging the renewal inherent in life, as well as the powerful influence of the forces of nature.

Key point

Two deaths of young men frame the play: that of Coral and Roy's son (who died before the play begins), and the inevitable, untimely death of Tom, which will happen after the play has finished. The play does not choose to show or even explore these deaths, but rather to deal with how death affects those who live.

Materialism and conformity

Key quotes

'We've got a new caravan. Everything in it you could want.' (Gwen, p.10)

'They shouldn't be going on a holiday if they can't afford one.' (Gwen, p.11)

'They have no right to behave any differently.' (Gwen, p.11)

'We were thinking of approaching Council to build us a proper brick and cement structure. Toilets, showers and a small shop selling essentials, hot food.' (First Camper, p.35)

'*GWEN staggers in with more things. MEG takes them from her and goes out.*' (p.56)

From early in the play, Gow addresses the issues of materialism and conformity. Gwen's snobbery and materialistic nature is shown early, with her bragging about the new caravan her family has purchased and through the insults she directs towards Tom and his family. In many ways her attitudes can be seen as representative of the attitudes of some people who made it through the Great Depression and rose to the ranks of the middle class when Australia experienced the relative affluence and stability of the 1950s. When Meg discovers that Gwen has left Jim's gift behind on purpose, Gwen shifts the argument and blame onto Meg's behaviour rather than admit she might find Jim's gift too menial.

Other characters, such as the Campers, can also be seen to reinforce notions of attachment to materialism and suburban conformity. The trivial concerns and complaints of the Campers represent those of people in Australian society who are unsatisfied with what they have, and who not only push for more but also put pressure on others to feel unsatisfied so as to gain support for their own narrow values and beliefs. The calm, unperturbed way in which Jim listens to their petty grievances, and then tears their petition into pieces once they have left, embodies the play's overall lack of sympathy for viewpoints that are inward-looking, selfish and intolerant of difference.

Although for most of the play Gwen seems to be aligned to these views and values, the storm brings her attachment to materialism to an end and, now stripped of material objects, she must embrace change. The final mime sequence in the penultimate scene of the play sees Gwen staggering in under the weight of her possessions, only to have Meg take away her 'baggage' and her over-attachment to objects, helping her to embrace a new life and perspective.

Journeys and the healing power of nature

Key quotes

'You going away tomorrow?' (Tom, p.4)

'It's a wonderful place. And what a piece of luck you found it.' (Vic, p.42)

'I think we should go for a walk ... Us girls. Along the water ... Just a stroll. Come on.' (Vic, p.44)

'You don't belong here. You must return to your own world and your own people ... Go back to the land, the grass, the sand.' (Tom, p.55)

'... it is the struggle between man and nature, as well as between man and man, and between man and himself that make this [*King Lear*] for me, his masterwork.' (Miss Latrobe, p.56)

The real plot of *Away* starts with Tom's question to Meg: 'You going away tomorrow?' This question introduces one of the central themes and premises of the play: the idea that going 'away' from one's habitual space (both literal and psychological) can help bring about growth and discovery.

Journeys become the central metaphor of the whole play, as suggested by the title. The play centres not just on the physical journey of going away – the annual tradition of Australian families going away for Christmas, to the beach – but also on the ways in which people can move 'away' from their own values, assumptions and preoccupations. In doing so, whether on their own initiative or in response to external events or others' influence, characters in *Away* are able to discover or rediscover themselves. For Gwen and Coral, the journeys are both physical and emotional; for both these characters too, the healing power of nature plays a significant role in their experience.

Other characters also represent different aspects of journeys. The Campers represent Australian suburban antagonism towards those who wish to undertake a journey beyond their norms and familiar comforts. They reject the notion of someone undertaking a journey to change or simply experience an adventure. Although we could see Gwen and Jim easily aligning with the Campers' values and ideas, Jim's refusal to sign the petition foreshadows him and his family embracing the physical and metaphysical journey that follows. The storm acts as a reason or catalyst for them to undertake a journey into uncharted territories and is a metaphor for the healing power of nature. Although the storm itself is destructive and disturbing, what follows is a sense of calm and the transition by many characters into a new stage of peace with each other and within themselves.

Gow's stage directions that after the storm '*there is darkness*' and then that the '*light becomes warm and intense*' attempt to portray nature as transformational through the use of the theatrical convention of lighting. Symbolically this creates the sense that it is only in light that transformation can happen. The action, from this point, primarily takes place outdoors (except perhaps for the concert, which the stage direction 'MC *appears in a spot*' suggests is performed indoors, p.52) and the forces of nature are allowed to light the way to the transformation of many characters.

Gwen is transformed through hearing about Tom's tragic circumstances, along with her walk on the beach and a swim in the sea. Coral's interaction with Tom, her performance of the play about the Sailor and the Mermaid, and the bonfire on the beach, help to heal and transform her. Roy burying his face in seashells in Coral's hands shows that he also has embraced transformation, partly through a connection with nature.

The end of the play implies that, although a superficial life can be chosen by individuals, to truly understand oneself, obstacles and hardships must be overcome, because it is the obstacles which nature places before us that ultimately lead to a greater understanding of self. In a class outdoors 'under the trees' in the morning, the final chapter of Tom's journey 'toward death' is alluded to, with the outdoor setting pointing to the absence of artifice and illusion in our search for deeper understanding and acceptance.

Key point

In her introduction first written for the 1988 Currency Press edition of Gow's *Away*, May-Brit Akerholt states: 'The quest undertaken by the characters in *Away* brings them home to the same old world but with a renewed sense of reality.' This sense of renewal is strong in the world of the characters in 1967, it was strong when the play was first performed in the 1980s and it is still strong today.

The symbolism of the beach

Key quotes

'I hope no one expects to take any of my good towels down onto the beach.' (Gwen, p.15)

'Look, they're all down on the beach already.' (Gwen, p.29)

'What about going round to the next beach?' (Harry, p.41)

'Sometimes when it's really hot it's nice to slip your bathers off in the water and just swim about like a fish.' (Vic, p.42)

The beach has been, ever since the beginning of the twentieth century, an iconic and dominant image in Australian culture and the Australian psyche. It appears in films, photographs, postcards and novels, and is one of the significant spaces of Australian identity, alongside 'the bush'.

The Australian beach started to become iconic in the nineteenth century with the paintings of Tom Roberts (*Slumbering Sea, Mentone*) and Charles Conder (*Sketch of Littlehampton Beach*). Paintings such as these portray the beach as an idyllic location where people may step out of their everyday working lives and enjoy a carefree and rejuvenating connection with nature. This mythology continued in the 1930s and 1940s through the photographs of Ray Leighton (*Boys and the Boards, Manly Beach, New South Wales*) and Max Dupain (*Sunbaker* and *Form at Bondi*). The 1979 novel *Puberty Blues* by Gabrielle Carey and Kathy Lette also helped to cement the beach in the Australian psyche. This notion of the beach giving Australians a sense of identity and place gained some academic credibility when it was discussed by Fiske, Hodge and Turner in their 1987 book *Myths of Oz*.

In the Australian psyche the beach is a holiday location, a tourist space and a place to experience a 'sea change'. It is characterised in Australian culture as everything from a hedonistic paradise to a place of withdrawal and healing. The beach in Australian history and culture has become a symbol of egalitarian ideals, a place removed from class, gender and racial divides. It is seen not just as a specific location but also as the space between two different natural elements – the land and the sea. Boundaries between two physical realities are often symbolically representative of change and growth, since such connections or intersections can demand negotiation and adaptation. *Away* begins in an unidentified town or suburb but it is once characters have taken the physical journey to the beach that they start to change emotionally, psychologically and spiritually. The beach becomes a place of transformation and healing.

Gwen, like the Campers her husband encounters, initially comes to the beach with all her baggage. These physical items can be seen as a symbol for her prejudices, snobbery and attachment to material objects. The storm brings discord to her control over the world; the storm, nature and serendipity (along with her daughter Meg's insistence) cause Gwen and her family to end up at the same beach as Tom's family. Gwen initially still tries to allow her snobbery and prejudices to be in charge but, in the experience of going for a walk and a swim with Vic, the power of the beach takes over – to the point where Gwen relinquishes her habitual control and even loses the sense of what she is feeling.

It is Gwen who leads the thunderous applause for Coral and Tom at the end of their performance of *The Stranger on the Shore*, signalling her emotional release. The beach acts as a catalyst for a new equity and freedom, which Gwen embraces; it allows her to let go and welcome a new life with her family, free of expectations and plans.

Coral is initially shown as a victim of her own grief, paralysed because of the death of her son. Like the marine invertebrate she is named after, Coral is vulnerable. When Roy asks her to behave normally and threatens her with shock therapy and institutionalisation, Coral hitchhikes away from the Gold Coast hotel and ends up at the beach where Tom and his family are staying.

Unlike Gwen, who eventually discards material objects when she arrives at this beach, Coral lets go of less tangible habits: she discards her grief and her whole identity and adopts the persona of 'the artist on the beach'. In the performance of *The Stranger on the Shore*, Coral achieves some acceptance of life and learns to 'walk' again. Her spirit then burns bright in the light of the bonfire on the beach.

Key point

The play involves the physical and emotional journeys of going 'away'; the beach serves as the setting for most of the play as well as the impetus for psychological, social and emotional changes in the characters. The beach becomes both the place of renewal and the stimulus or driving force behind this renewal.

Shakespearean parallels

Key quotes

'Give me your hands, if we be friends, / And Robin shall restore amends.' (p.3)

'Meantime we shall express our darker purpose.' (p.57)

'... while we / Unburden'd crawl toward death.' (p.57)

Although Shakespearean allusion is not a theme in itself, *Away* creates significant parallels with Shakespearean texts, and this is an important source of ideas and meaning in the play. Shakespearean drama is much more than an intertextual reference in *Away*. The world of Shakespeare's plays frames *Away* from a narrative, stylistic and theatrical perspective. In this sense, Gow can be seen to be attempting to engage his audience with the notion of theatre as a universal art which transcends time.

Stylistically, by bookending *Away* with Shakespeare's *A Midsummer Night's Dream* in the opening and *King Lear* at the end, Gow creates a sense of magic realism – everyday events and the real-world setting of the play are stylised by fantastical elements – and this serves to heighten the dramatic intensity. Unlike many other Australian playwrights of the 1970s and 1980s, Gow frames his play within non-naturalism rather than naturalism. He even uses a theatrical convention that is frequently seen in Shakespeare's works: the notion of using a play within a play. Within *Away*, three plays or sections of plays are performed: the last scene of *A Midsummer Night's Dream*, the playlet of *The Stranger on the Shore* and Lear's first speech from *King Lear*.

Besides framing his play within the conventions and 'world' of Shakespeare's plays, Gow also references *A Midsummer Night's Dream* and *King Lear* in other ways to create intertextuality. This means that allusions to other texts may be made through characters, actions and events, and not simply through the reproduction of dialogue from another play. For example, when Tom performs Puck's final speech from *A Midsummer Night's Dream* at the beginning of *Away*, a parallel is created between Puck and Tom, and the events of the play develop this parallel in various ways. Tom, as Puck, promises to 'restore amends' if the audience applauds, and he does achieve this. Tom, like Puck, becomes a magical or transformational force, helping other characters to embrace their own realities and rebuild damaged relationships.

The movement of the play from the domestic world of the characters to the unfamiliar and magical world of the beach echoes the movement from the world of the court to the magical world of the forest in *A Midsummer Night's Dream*. As with Shakespeare's characters in the forest, the fears and inhibitions of characters in *Away* seem to dissipate when they are finally at the beach. This suggests that in Gow's play the beach symbolically represents the world of the unconscious.

Gow uses intertextuality to add layers of meaning throughout the play. The Shakespearean references create a tragicomic mood but then Gow plays with these references through unexpected twists, such as having Tom and Meg become friends rather than lovers and hinting at some darker tragedy surrounding Tom without revealing it initially. The re-entrance of the Fairies to create the storm, along with the appearance of a mysterious woman in a kaftan (Coral), are moments of sheer fantasy which come at the most dramatic points, just before Tom's cancer is revealed.

The play ends at the beginning of the next school year, when Miss Latrobe has taken her students outside to read Shakespeare. Here, Gow is echoing the circular narrative evident in some Shakespearean comedies, but he once again plays with the expectation created by such an echo when he unexpectedly reveals the play being read to be one of Shakespeare's darkest tragedies – *King Lear*. Tom is asked to read Lear's opening speech, with its ominous first line: 'Meantime we shall express our darker purpose'.

A sense of tragedy and foreboding thus hangs over the end of the play, in contrast to the audience's possible expectations of a satisfying resolution in the manner of Shakespeare's comedies.

DIFFERENT INTERPRETATIONS

Different interpretations arise from different responses to a text. Over time, a text will give rise to a wide range of responses from its readers, who may come from various social or cultural groups and live in very different places and historical periods. Responses by critics and reviewers can be published in newspapers, journals and books, both online and in print. They can also be expressed in discussions among readers in the media, classrooms, book groups and so on.

While there is no single correct reading or interpretation of a text, it is important to understand that an interpretation is more than a personal opinion – it is the justification of a point of view on the text. To present an interpretation of a text based on your point of view, you must use a logical argument and support it with relevant evidence from the text.

The critics' viewpoints

Away was a critical, popular and financial success when it was first performed. Director Peter Kingston's original production struck a note with critics and Sydney audiences in 1986 at the Stables Theatre for many reasons. The play seemed fresh, familiar and truthful. Part of its authenticity came from the fact that Gow set the play in Australia in the summer of 1967–68, a context he knew from his childhood. Other elements were also easily recognised, such as the Shakespearean references and allusions, and familiar stereotypes. But even the original critics and audiences realised that this play, grounded in reality, did more. It exposed the relationships, values and behaviours of ordinary Australians as flawed and claustrophobic and created a poignant landscape in which deep self-awareness and transformation could be seen to prevail.

The play's classical structure pleased some critics in 1987 but was considered too formal by others. Some thought the use of conventions such as magic realism was innovative while others felt that these would make the play date quickly. The classical structure Gow used – along with his selective use of Shakespearean allusions and magic realism – seems to have endured, helping the play to seem universal while remaining contemporary and accessible. Gow integrates these techniques in order to explore a diverse range of themes and ideas, from family rituals to materialism, intolerance and conformity, to the healing power of nature.

With specific reference to the Shakespearean elements of the play, the theatre critic HG Kippax believed that the parallels with the Shakespearean texts made the play's message of regeneration emerge (Kippax 1987). Conversely Elizabeth Webby, another critic of the original 1987 production, saw the Shakespearean intertextuality as being forced and adding to an audience's sense of disorientation (Webby 1993). However, audiences took to the play and related to the characters and themes presented.

Tom and Coral are two of the most important characters in *Away* and, when the play opened in 1987, they seemed to capture the minds of critics and the hearts of audiences. It could be argued that this was due to the wide age range of audiences at the Stables Theatre, which included members of both Tom's and Coral's generations who could identify directly with these characters. Had the play first been performed in front of less diverse audiences it might have been pigeonholed as having a narrow appeal and might not have had the opportunity to prove its broader relevance. But other factors also seem to be at work.

The play's setting at a pivotal time of social and political change in Australia, along with the clarity with which Gow portrays social differences, give it greater gravity. Gwen's snobbery and attachment to material objects, contrasted with the open egalitarian attitudes represented by Tom's family, gave rise to sociological critiques of *Away* during in the late 1980s and early 1990s which ensured the play would continue to stimulate discussion. However, as the study of psychology has become increasingly popular in universities and schools in the early twenty-first century, psychoanalytic interpretations of *Away* have become more widespread. So, in addition to its continuing social relevance, the play also invites analyses and interpretations on a more intimate and interpersonal scale.

Perhaps it is the universality of the play's ideas, themes and characters that has allowed it to endure and change and become a favourite for major theatre company revivals, amateur drama groups, school and university study and high-school productions.

Two interpretations

The following discussion shows how two contrasting interpretations of *Away* can be supported by logical argument and carefully selected textual evidence.

Interpretation 1

***Away* shows the battle and the eventual triumph of egalitarian working-class values over materialism and middle-class values.**

Interpretations that concentrate on the political and social contexts of the play and its characters are useful for examining the views and values inherent in the text. Gow's play presents many social classes and the ruling or dominant classes are not portrayed as privileged or triumphing. This interpretation would see the play as essentially a drama which shows a class struggle whereby the values of the working class, as represented by Tom's family, battle against and triumph over the middle-class attitudes and values reflected in Meg's family and by Coral and Roy.

A sociological analysis addressing the social and political context presented in the play would put emphasis on the fact that, stylistically, the play begins like a satire of suburban banality. Three families (two of which are easily identified as middle class) meet after a school play and talk about and compare their plans for the summer holidays. The scene, set against the apparent innocence of the 1960s, initially seems to be nostalgic, but by the second act irony becomes apparent, as each of the families is shown to be fractured by its own conflicts and challenges, and eventually Gow unleashes a social satire. Gow's strength as a dramatic writer seems to come from his ability to portray and analyse the experiences of the lower-middle-class families.

An interpretation that concentrates on the social and political perspectives in the play can help us to analyse the way that Gow uses *Away* to critique Australian society's preoccupation, during the post–World War II period and also in more recent times, with materialism and social advancement at the cost of equality. In this sense, Roy and Gwen would be seen as the representatives of bourgeois attitudes and the dangers of the materialism evident in Australia, especially in the 1950s and early 1960s. Tom and Meg would be seen as agents for change, a younger generation not concerned with class or materialism. Coral would be seen as the first person of the older generation to consciously accept liberation from her class as she 'walks' in a world free from the sacrifices of the past and the threat of institutionalisation.

The narrative of the play reveals the interconnectedness of people from different classes, and endorses the ultimate triumph of egalitarian working-class values over the willingness to conform to conservative social expectations or blind materialism. This is portrayed by:

- Gwen's snobbery and attitude towards Tom and his family
- Roy's over-concern with social appearance and status
- Gwen's materialism and control and the way it almost destroys her family
- the Campers' complaints, which typify the prejudices of small-minded bourgeois Australian attitudes – and are dismissed so easily by Jim tearing up the petition
- the fact that Tom and his family's egalitarian values dominate at the end of the play.

Interpretation 2

***Away* presents three families in crisis and suggests that physical and emotional transformations cannot occur until psychological shifts take place.**

While *Away* addresses important social and political concerns, it can also be read as a study of the interpersonal dynamics in three families. The journeys of the various characters show how key psychological issues contribute to growth, resolution, acceptance and change.

Away starts with Tom performing Puck's last speech from Shakespeare's *A Midsummer Night's Dream*. This gives Gow's drama a dreamlike context. The play follows the experiences of three families in crisis as they go 'away' for the summer holidays and, from a psychological perspective, this represents the journey of these families and characters away from what is familiar, towards what is transformational.

One family faces a crisis as a result of external forces, in the form of the son having been killed in the Vietnam War. Another family faces an emotional crisis in the form of the disintegration of relationships due to a wife and mother's controlling behaviour and expectations, under the guise of care and love. The third family faces a more insidious and hidden crisis in the form of the son's life-threatening illness. Each of the characters must face the deeply personal challenges that threaten to destroy their own family unit, and each of them undertakes a different journey of discovery during the play, learning from others and experiencing psychological shifts that allow them to move forward emotionally.

The grief-stricken Coral, for example, suffers an inability to move beyond the trauma of losing her son. She is trapped in a world of her own, feels disconnected from her husband, and cannot relate to those around her in ways that make sense to them. Roy's desire to return his wife to 'normality', even at the expense of institutionalising her and subjecting her to 'shock treatment', can be seen as evidence of his own response to grief – he, too, has refused to come to terms with the loss of his son. Neither knows how to support the other in their suffering.

It is not until they both experience psychological shifts during the holiday 'away' that they can begin to reconcile with their past and with each other, beginning to move towards an emotional transition into a time of healing. This is symbolised by the exchange of seashells near the end of the play.

Psychological perspectives of *Away*, while generating more character-based readings of the play, can still encompass broader social issues raised by relationships and events. For instance, Gwen is portrayed as a stereotypical harassed housewife who denies herself an identity outside of her family. This can be seen to reinforce the identity that some women create for themselves, whereby their own needs are made secondary to the needs of others and the expectations placed upon them by others.

Conversely, Coral can be seen as a representation of femininity which is bound up in notions of a woman being determined by her emotional world and seeking salvation through masculine figures. It is interesting that Coral is able to psychologically liberate herself from her emotional world and gender stereotypes as she learns to 'walk' on her own again.

Gwen and Coral present quite different social ideals of femininity, and the play argues that neither is fully attainable or even desirable. Both suffer when they attempt to fulfil these particular roles, and only achieve an emotional transformation when they find ways to overcome the psychological challenges created by their perceptions of society's expectations.

A number of other elements in *Away* can also be looked at through a psychological lens, further developing this reading of the play. You might consider:

- the main characters in terms of archetypes
- Tom's psychological function as a healer of other characters
- Coral asking men whether she looks like Kim Novak, which alludes to the notion that some women see themselves in terms of representations of female identities in the media

- Coral's attraction to younger men who are like her son, which has sexual dimensions as well as being indicative of her inability to deal with mortality
- Roy's desire for his wife to be 'normal' according to social expectations
- Gwen's desire for material satisfaction, for external approval and for people to see her as important
- Tom's desire for sexual fulfilment and procreation.

QUESTIONS & ANSWERS

This section focuses on your own analytical writing on the text, and gives you strategies for producing high-quality responses in your coursework and exam essays.

Essay writing – an overview

An essay on a literary work is a formal and serious piece of writing that presents your point of view on the text, usually in response to a given topic. Your 'point of view' in an essay is your interpretation of the meaning of the text's language, structure, characters, situations and events, supported by detailed analysis of textual evidence.

Analyse – don't summarise

In your essays it is important to avoid simply summarising what happens in a text.

- A **summary** is a description or paraphrase (retelling in different words) of the characters and events. For example: 'Macbeth has a horrifying vision of a dagger dripping with blood before he goes to murder King Duncan.'
- An **analysis** is an explanation of the real meaning or significance that lies 'beneath' the text's words (and images, for a film). For example: 'Macbeth's vision of a bloody dagger shows how deeply uneasy he is about the violent act he is contemplating – as well as his sense that supernatural forces are impelling him to act.'

A limited amount of summary is sometimes necessary to let your reader know which part of the text you wish to discuss. However, always keep this to a minimum and follow it immediately with your analysis of what this part of the text is really telling us.

Plan your essay

Carefully plan your essay so that you have a clear idea of what you are going to say. The plan ensures that your ideas flow logically, that your argument remains consistent and that you stay on the topic. An essay plan should be a list of **brief dot points** – no more than half a page.

- Include your central argument or main contention – a concise statement (usually in a single sentence) of your overall response to the topic.
- Write three or four dot points for each paragraph indicating the main idea and evidence/examples from the text. Note that in your essay you will need to *expand* on these points and *analyse* the evidence.

Structure your essay

An essay is a complete, self-contained piece of writing. It has a clear beginning (the introduction), middle (several body paragraphs) and end (the last paragraph or conclusion). It must also have a central argument that runs throughout, linking each paragraph to form a coherent whole.

The introduction establishes your overall response to the topic. It includes your main contention and outlines the main evidence you will refer to in the course of the essay. Write your introduction *after* you have done a plan and *before* you write the rest of the essay.

The body paragraphs argue your case – they present evidence from the text and explain how this evidence supports your argument. Each body paragraph needs:

- **a strong topic sentence** (usually the first sentence) that states the main point being made in the paragraph
- **evidence** from the text, including some brief quotations
- **analysis** of the textual evidence explaining its significance and **explanation** of how it supports your argument
- **links back to the topic** in one or more statements, usually towards the end of the paragraph.

Connect the body paragraphs so that your discussion flows smoothly. Use some linking words and phrases such as 'similarly' and 'on the other hand', though don't start every paragraph like this. Another strategy is to use a significant word from the last sentence of one paragraph in the first sentence of the next.

Use key terms from the topic – or synonyms for them – throughout, so the relevance of your discussion to the topic is always clear.

The conclusion ties everything together and finishes the essay. It includes strong statements that emphasise your central argument and provide a clear response to the topic.

Avoid simply restating the points made earlier in the essay – this will end on a very flat note and imply that you have run out of ideas and vocabulary. The conclusion is meant to be a logical extension of what you have written, not just a repetition or summary. Writing an effective conclusion can be a challenge. Try using these tips:

- Start by linking back to the final sentence of the second-last paragraph – this helps your writing to 'flow', rather than leaping back to your main contention straight away.
- Use synonyms and expressions with equivalent meanings to vary your vocabulary. This allows you to reinforce your line of argument without being repetitive.
- When planning your essay, think of one or two broad statements or observations about the text's wider meaning. These should be related to the topic and your overall argument. Keep them for the conclusion, since they will give you something 'new' to say but still follow logically from your discussion. The introduction will be focused on the topic, but the conclusion can present a wider view of the text.

Essay topics

1. 'Both Tom and Coral are the heroes of *Away* since their lives encourage changes in others.' Do you agree?
2. '*Away* juxtaposes realistic characters and situations with stereotypes and unreal happenings for the purpose of exploring both individuals and society.' Discuss.
3. "Still waters stink." '*Away* is a play that advocates change and warns of the dangers of standing still.' Discuss.
4. How do intertextuality and cultural references help convey the themes in *Away*?
5. '*Away* is a play more about the transformational forces of nature than the ability of humans to transform themselves.' Discuss.
6. "We don't look back and we don't look forward." To what extent does *Away* endorse the value of living in the present?
7. How does Michael Gow use dramatic conventions to explore human relationships and concepts of change in *Away*?
8. '*Away* is a play about the transformational power of undertaking a journey.' Discuss.
9. '*Away* is about the strength that some people find when challenged by adversity.' Do you agree?
10. Is *Away* ultimately an optimistic or a pessimistic play?

Vocabulary for writing on *Away*

Bex: In the play, Gwen constantly refers to needing to 'take a Bex'. Bex was a 1960s medicinal powder that contained aspirin and caffeine and was taken mostly by women. 'Have a cup of tea, a Bex and a good lie down' was the slogan used in advertisements for Bex in the 1960s when it was marketed as a cure for many ailments.

Chips Rafferty: Chips Rafferty was a successful Australian film actor in the 1940s to 1960s who was seen by many of the period as a symbol of a 'typical Australian'. He appeared in commercials in Britain in the 1950s to encourage British people to migrate to Australia.

Deus ex machina: This Latin phrase, literally 'God from a machine', is the term for an unexpected or improbable theatrical device to unravel the plot.

Dramatic irony: In theatre, this is when the meaning or purpose of an action, situation or speech is understood by the audience but not understood by a character or characters in the play.

Greek chorus: In ancient Greek theatre the Chorus was a group of performers who spoke, sang and/or danced in unison as a collective voice representing the general population, to tell the story or comment on the action or themes in the play. In *Away*, as in some ancient Greek comedies, the Campers' comments can be seen to present a collective viewpoint while ironically commenting on the views they express.

Kim Novak: Kim Novak (b. 1933) is an American film actress best known for her sexy screen image in films of the 1950s and 1960s. Often she played the *femme fatale* or 'siren-like' role. Coral compares herself to Kim Novak on a number of occasions.

Magic realism: A movement in art and theatre that uses fantastical elements or events and places them in a real-world setting. Often the purpose of this is to add a heightened sense of mystery or intensity, as well as creating dramatic emphasis for important moments in the play. Gow uses stylistic elements of magic realism at the climax of the play when the Fairies stage a 'spectacular storm' and just before Tom's cancer is revealed.

Shakespearean allusions: A technique whereby a writer makes a direct reference to, or draws a parallel with, the events or characters in a Shakespearean play. In *Away*, Gow makes allusions to *A Midsummer Night's Dream*, *The Tempest* and *King Lear*.

Analysing a sample topic

"Still waters stink." '*Away* is a play that advocates change and warns of the dangers of standing still.' Discuss.

- It is a good idea to begin the process of writing an essay by circling the focus words that define what you need to do, and underlining the key words. Here you would circle 'discuss', which indicates that you need to try to cover the issues raised and not just address one side or viewpoint. Also underline any key words in the prompt statement: 'advocates', 'change', 'warns', 'dangers' and 'standing still'.
- Take a moment to think what is meant by this question/statement in relation to the text. Jot down synonyms for the key words. Write down any examples or quotes from the text you think may be appropriate.
- Identify the different aspects of the statement and make notes about your main arguments. Remember, since this statement asks you to discuss, you will need to provide more than one viewpoint or argument.
- Look closely at what the statement is asserting: that if people stay still they become stagnant and that the play actively promotes change as a way out of this stagnancy. Consider how you are going to define stillness and change. You need to form your own opinion at this point and write it down.
- Write down four to six arguments you would make to prove your contention then list the examples or evidence from the text that support these arguments.

Sample introduction

When Meg says to Tom that 'Still waters run deep', he replies that 'Still waters stink'. In this sense, Gow is advocating, through Tom's response, a major message of the play: that people who stay still (are unable to change) become stagnant and cannot continue to live a productive life. In the opening scene of *Away*, Tom, playing Puck in *A Midsummer Night's Dream*, promises to 'restore amends'. Gow's use of Shakespearean allusions throughout the play gives resonance to the restorative influence that Tom has on all those around him. It is through change and transformation that the characters are able to 'restore amends', to escape the stagnancy of their lives and to move forward to a more hopeful future.

Body paragraphs

The following pieces of textual evidence and reasoning could be used to develop the discussion in the body paragraphs.

- The play centres not just on the physical journey of going away but also on the premise that it is by going away from oneself and the preconceptions and values that one holds dear that we are able to truly discover or rediscover ourselves and others.
- Many characters, such as Gwen and Coral, undergo journeys that involve physical, emotional and psychological changes.
- Tom's cancer has brought his parents on a journey to question what they value most in life and this causes them to treasure the precious time they have left with their son.
- Some of the secondary characters in the play represent different attitudes to transformation. The Campers reject the notion of someone undertaking a journey to change.
- The storm literally and metaphorically acts as a catalyst for Harry and his family to release themselves from stagnancy and undertake a journey into uncharted territories.
- The play ends with Tom, who has facilitated transformation and change in others, having to finally undergo a journey in which he will face the great struggle between himself and nature as he prepares for his 'unburden'd crawl toward death'.

Sample conclusion

Away explores some of the ways in which people can become stagnant when they try to avoid, or deny, changes in their lives, as well as the consequences for both themselves and those close to them. It shows how preconceptions and emotional stasis can prevent discovery and renewal. In the early parts of the play, we see how such stagnancy can inhibit relationships, generate conflict and contribute to suffering. As events unfold, they offer evidence that transformation – while sometimes difficult – provides a path towards reconciliation and growth. It is through undergoing a journey that physical, emotional and psychological changes occur, and these changes in turn enable individuals to address personal crises and to move towards more loving and fulfilling lives.

SAMPLE ANSWER

'*Away* is a play about the transformational power of undertaking a journey.' Discuss.

Michael Gow's 1987 play *Away* is set in the summer of 1968 at a crucial point of change in Australian history. It is a time when Australia is at a crossroads and is forced to question its identity as a nation, realising that its Eurocentric and isolationist foreign policies can no longer continue. The play uses this setting to explore the transformational journey of three families as they move from the isolation of their own world towards a connection with themselves, others and the world at large.

The play opens with the character Tom performing Puck's final speech from *A Midsummer Night's Dream*. Tom as Puck promises to 'restore amends' if the audience applauds and this establishes Tom from the outset as a transformational force who will take other characters on a journey towards their true selves and towards love and forgiveness. The movement of the play from the domestic world of the characters to the unfamiliar and magical world of the beach has parallels in the movement from the world of the court to the magical world of the forest in *A Midsummer Night's Dream* and it is this physical transformation which facilitates more fundamental psychological and emotional transformations in the characters in *Away*.

In Act One, Scene Two, Tom asks Meg, 'You going away tomorrow?' This literal question touches on one of the central thematic concerns of the play – the notion of journey. The play centres on the annual cultural event of Australian families going away for Christmas to the beach. Going 'away' also becomes the central metaphor of the whole play as well as its title. The play centres not just on the physical journey of going away but also on the premise that it is by going away from our familiar routines and contexts that we are able to truly discover ourselves and others. Many characters, such as Gwen and Coral, undergo transformational physical, emotional and psychological journeys.

The choice of the summer holiday as the catalyst for the journey and transformation of the characters makes the play both familiar and potent for an audience. Going away on a summer holiday is a time for families to relax outside of the constraints of their everyday environment. In *Away*, Coral and Roy are still mourning the loss of their son; Gwen, Jim and Meg are constantly fighting; and Vic, Harry and Tom need an escape from the overshadowing inevitability of Tom's death.

The physical journey of these characters takes on greater resonance when the healing power of nature intervenes. The tempest or storm metaphorically strips away Gwen's sense of her own self. This combines with the cleansing properties of walking on the beach and swimming in the water, as well as the devastating news of Tom's terminal illness, to transform Gwen. She initially loses her sense of feeling but eventually grows to embrace and accept her family.

After being threatened with shock treatment and institutionalisation by her husband, Coral turns up as the mysterious woman in a kaftan at the beach where Tom and his family are holidaying. This second meeting with Tom seems to bring about a healing process in Coral which reaches its catharsis in the playlet they perform and the bonfire on the beach. Her final action – pouring shells through her hands – symbolises her acceptance of her son's death and of mortality as a force of nature which must be acknowledged, not denied. Roy burying his face in seashells in Coral's hands shows that he also has embraced transformation and nature.

The fact that the play comes full circle back to Shakespeare gives a sense of completion of a journey after transformation has occurred. The play ends at the beginning of the next school year when Miss Latrobe has taken her students outside to read Shakespeare's *King Lear*. Tom is asked to read Lear's opening speech, 'Meantime we shall express our darker purpose.'

The play has seen Tom transform and 'heal' others (especially Coral and Gwen) but he now faces his own journey towards acceptance of his own death. This class is held outside 'under the trees' in natural light and this implies some sense of hope for Tom as he finally undertakes this journey. It also raises the broader concerns of the journey of *Away*: all the characters in the play have had to confront issues of life, death and human nature and, after having been 'away' and transformed, they now 'unburden'd crawl toward death'.

REFERENCES & READING

Text

Gow, Michael 2012, *Away*, Currency Press, Strawberry Hills, Australia. First published in 1986.

Further reading

Akerholt, May-Brit 1988, 'Michael Gow talks to May-Brit Akerholt', *Australasian Drama Studies*, no. 12–13.

Bramwell, Murray 2006, 'Coming Home to Away', http://murraybramwell.com/?p–1631

Fiske, John, Hodge, Bob & Turner, Graeme 1987, *Myths of Oz: Reading Australian Popular Culture*, Allen & Unwin, Sydney.

Kippax, HG 1987, Review of *Away*, *The Sydney Morning Herald*, 2 May, p.4.

Radvan, Helen 1988, *Away Teachers Kit*, La Boite Theatre Education Unit, Brisbane.

Simon, Luke 1991, *Michael Gow's Plays*, Currency Press, Strawberry Hills, Sydney.

Stubbings, J 1996, 'Still waters run deep', *The Age Student Update*, 11 March, p.10.

Webby, Elizabeth 1993, *Modern Australian Plays*, Sydney University Press, Sydney, pp.55–6.